LORRAINE

LORRAINE

THE BIOGRAPHY OF TV'S BEST-LOVED PRESENTER

NEIL SIMPSON

JOHN BLAKE

Published by John Blake Publishing Ltd,
3 Bramber Court, 2 Bramber Road,
London W14 9PB, England

www.blake.co.uk

First published in hardback in 2007

ISBN 978 1 84454 384 7

British Library Cataloguing-in-Publication Data:

A catalogue record for this book is available from the British Library.

Design by www.envydesign.co.uk

Printed and bound in Great Britain by William Clowes Ltd, Beccles, Suffolk

1 3 5 7 9 10 8 6 4 2

Papers used by John Blake Publishing are natural, recyclable products
made from wood grown in sustainable forests. The manufacturing processes
conform to the environmental regulations of the country of origin.

Every attempt has been made to contact the relevant copyright-holders,
but some were unobtainable. We would be grateful if the appropriate
people could contact us.

CONTENTS

INTRODUCTION

'Hi there, good morning – welcome to LK Today.'

I t is exactly 8.35am and Lorraine Kelly will be in front of five cameras at the London Television Centre for the next fifty minutes. All around her, the show's twelve-strong production crew in the studio and the galleries will dart and dash, mouthing instructions, checking timings and dealing with all the usual last-minute panics. But at the centre of the storm Lorraine herself will be as calm and cheerful as she has been for every one of the past twenty-one years she has spent in the early morning spotlight. She smiles as her favourite make-up lady leaps forward to pat her face and hair during the commercial breaks. She reassures nervous guests and holds their hands just before their big moment on screen. She gets more facts from the show's resident experts before interviewing them on the big feature of the day. And when the cameras roll, she makes sure that there are no silences, no continuity breaks and no over-runs on what is still the most popular late-morning television show in the country.

'We're going to take a very quick break now but there'll be a lot more when we come back.' The first commercials normally come just under twelve minutes into the programme and Lorraine is already setting a cracking pace. A celebrity guest, a topical reference, a fashion show, a true-life crisis. Lorraine moves seamlessly from one to the next, with just a quick glance down at the paperwork on the desk in front of her as she switches her gaze from one red-lit camera to another. The autocue is rolling but everyone knows Lorraine could manage just fine without it.

'That's all we have time for – see you tomorrow.'

With a final smile at the main camera, Lorraine and the crew see their live transmission cut out. Another show is over. Lorraine sits back momentarily in her chair, looking upwards and off-set towards the gantry of ugly iron girders and lights that the viewers never get to see. There is always a flash of relief, a catching of breath when any live broadcast ends. But for Lorraine her day's work is far from done. She is soon disconnecting her earpiece and microphone and on her feet because her make-up lady needs to be thanked. Her relieved guests need to be congratulated for holding their nerves. Her resident experts need to be primed for their next appearances. And the whole production team needs to be assured that everything is still going well and that tomorrow's show will be even better.

'Doing an hour of live television every morning is no-where near as easy as it looks,' says breakfast television producer Anton Gray. 'Everything is planned down to the second but running orders can still change at any point. Some guests can talk too much and be impossible to shut up. Others can clam up totally because the whole experience is so nerve-wracking.

For a breakfast show to work, the presenter needs to be able to take control in either situation. She needs to connect with the viewer and keep talking if technical glitches hold up any pre-taped clips or segments. She needs to be able to look relaxed and keep chatting while hearing all hell breaking loose in her ear-piece.'

And when it comes to breakfast television nobody does all this like Lorraine.

She is famous for talking to politicians, celebrities, soap and music stars. She can interview grieving parents and traumatised youngsters. She can somehow speak for everybody because she has never kept her own hopes, fears or insecurities from her fans. She has opinions on everything from weight loss to the fame game and she's never been shy of passing them on. What makes Lorraine Kelly special is the sense that she really is just like the rest of us.

'She gets to talk to the kind of people we won't ever have access to. But when she does speak to them she asks them the same kind of questions that we would if we had the chance,' says television critic Charles Connolly. 'If she thinks fashions are ridiculous she will say so. If she thinks a diet is dangerous she'll tell us. If something is making her laugh she will share the joke. You feel as if she could pop out of your television, into your living room or kitchen and just carry on chatting like a fabulously gossipy old friend. She is ordinary, yet extraordinary at the same time. That's her gift.'

What also makes Lorraine a class apart from many of her broadcasting peers is her sheer longevity. She alone has outlasted all the other superstars of the breakfast television market. From Anne Diamond to Anthea Turner, from Roland Rat to Eamonn Holmes – Lorraine has sat alongside them all.

And she alone is still on the sofa today. Her enduring appeal and sheer professionalism helped her beat the likes of Jeremy Clarkson to the title of Presenter of the Year from the prestigious Royal Television Society in 2006 – some twenty-one years after she first appeared on screen with TV-am.

But what lies behind that appeal and professionalism? What exactly is it that has helped Lorraine Kelly to thrive when so many of her rivals have disappeared from our screens?

Those that know Lorraine well say that there can be steel behind her smile – but that she never pushes anyone as hard as she pushes herself. It is this steel which has taken her from the most unpromising of beginnings to become one of the best-paid women in British broadcasting. The steel that made her run her first marathon as a forty-three-year-old mum-of-one. The steel which has seen her quietly raise hundreds of thousands of pounds for literally dozens of charities – many of which say they have no more loyal supporter than the girl from the Gorbals who can never forget the poverty she saw all around her as a child.

Lorraine's friends also say she has always been a woman in a hurry. She was the first girl from her school to move into full-time work. She was the first from her circle of friends to scratch together enough money to buy her own flat. The first to move to London even though her heart has never left Scotland. They also say she has never lost her ability to surprise. The Lorraine Kelly they have all grown up with can stay up until 3am re-reading her beloved Russian literature. Yet she can still be on screen before 9am talking happily about a Hollywood starlet who has fallen out of her dress at an awards ceremony. They say the real Lorraine Kelly is actually as passionate about politics as she is about pop stars. When she recently told her husband and daughter that she wanted to pull a sledge 100 miles across the Antarctic neither of them batted an eyelid. It was just the kind of crazy plan they expected of her, she said. Like most of Lorraine's crazy plans it is one few people would bet against her achieving.

Joyce Woodrow first met Lorraine when they were two shy thirteen-year-olds at high school in East Kilbride. They have been the closest of friends ever since and Joyce says her pal has never let fame or fortune go to her head. 'I know that if I was in trouble and had to ring someone at 3am in the morning then Lorraine would be there for me, without question,' she says. Joyce also knows that if she wants to dance on a bar at a Paris nightclub at 3am then there is no better person to do it with than Lorraine – as the staff at the Whisky-a-GoGo club can attest, having seen the pair in action on one of their regular weekend breaks.

* * * * *

Whenever journalists ask Lorraine for the secret of her success she puts much of it down to luck. But in truth there is a whole lot more to it than that. Her giggles, her laughs and her gaffes might have helped make her famous. But television and radio insiders say there is a very serious side to her as well – industry legend says very few presenters prepare as thoroughly or work as hard as Lorraine Kelly. She has paid her dues on newspapers as well as on television. She has been surrounded by terrible tragedy, as well as genuine joy. This is her incredible story.

1

THE GIRL FROM
THE GORBALS

'Our next flat was luxury – it had an inside loo!'

Lorraine Kelly wasn't supposed to be born in a tenement block deep in the heart of Glasgow's infamous Gorbals estate. The tiny, one-room flat had no hot running water and the only toilet was several flights of stairs away in the brick-strewn backyard. Her parents, Anne and John, had moved in as seventeen-year-old newly-weds planning to use it as a stepping-stone to better things. They were so thrilled to be starting their new lives together that they didn't care about their surroundings. So what if most of the people on the local streets looked as if they had just been released from the nearby Barlinnie prison? So what if the south side of the River Clyde had already become one of Europe's biggest and most depressing slums? The Kellys were going to ignore all of that and turn their Ballater Street flat into the happiest and safest home in the city – and they succeeded.

John was an apprentice at a local electrical repair firm, specialising in televisions. There was plenty of work to be done and he was prepared to put in as many hours as necessary to learn the skills and make a success of his job. Televisions in the late 1950s were huge, unreliable and exciting beasts. John was going to have fun trying to tame them. Meanwhile, Anne had just got a job in a department store in the city centre – it was hard on the feet but it was a great place to spend the day. Always sociable, always ready with a smile and a laugh, she thrived on the relationships she was building up with her colleagues and customers.

Back in Ballater Street in the evenings the newly-weds couldn't have been happier. They shared the stories of their days and dreamed big dreams for the future. Elvis and Bobby Darin were on the radio and Britain finally seemed ready to break out of its endless post-war gloom. The country was even taking on Hollywood with its own film-star heart-throb – a handsome young singer going by the name of Cliff Richard, who Anne had little idea she would one day get to meet alongside her grown-up daughter. As the months passed Anne and John saved up enough to buy some better furniture and even had the occasional night out.

They also bought and borrowed a surprisingly large collection of books. Both were big readers, happily alternating from popular fiction to the classics – and while many of their books were second- or even third-hand, none were ever thrown away. Married life was good and their tenement block flat had indeed turned into a happy home for two. But, of course, the couple weren't to stay on their own for long. Within six months of getting married and walking up the stairs to the flat, Anne realised she was pregnant – she hadn't even turned eighteen. Looking back she says she was surprised, scared and excited all at once, and fortunately, John was thrilled. Neither of them had planned to start a family so soon, especially while in their tiny first home when money was still so tight, but they vowed to make it work.

As 1959 drew to a close the doctors said the Kelly's baby might be born on New Year's Day, the first day of the new decade and a true child of the sixties. But Anne started to feel labour pains a lot sooner. Her waters broke on the last day of November and she was rushed to Glasgow's Rottenrow Maternity Hospital. The same day, 30 November 1959, she gave birth to a daughter weighing just four and a half pounds – a child the family wanted to call Winifred. 'It was Winston Churchill's birthday,' she remembers. 'And my mother thought Winifred would be a fitting name to honour him with.'

But was that really the right name for the tiny little girl asleep in her mother's arms? Her parents decided it wasn't. Their daughter was to be Lorraine Kelly – and she has never stopped thanking them for the decision. 'They reckon you grow into your name, but I don't think I would have ever grown into a Winifred,' she said years later, when the near miss had become a long-standing family joke.

Astrologers suggest that Winifred Kelly could still have been an entertainer, however, because they say 30 November 1959 was the perfect day for a future celebrity to be born – even one with a ridiculous first name. A combination of Mars and Scorpio gave her a 'super-trouper showbiz aspect' according to one reading Winifred had, while the linking of the sun, the moon and Jupiter meant a fun-loving but frank Sagittarian mentality. She would be the kind of person to soldier on no matter what, often putting her own needs and feelings last to please others. 'Giving, generous and loyal, but not someone who suffers fools gladly – Mercury in Scorpio hinting of an acid tongue when crossed,' said another reading.

Lorraine also had a clear sense of humour from the start. 'I was a month early and weighed only four and a half pounds, but I've been making up for it ever since,' she jokes about her birth.

After leaving Rottenrow and heading back into the Gorbals the Kelly family tried to adapt their tiny flat to their new situation. Anne and John slept in a slightly recessed area set into the wall of the one main room, Lorraine in a tiny cot right next to them. She learned to walk and talk surrounded by love and family. There was poverty all around them, but there were few happier or more cared-for babies.

* * * * *

When Lorraine was two her parents had finally saved up enough money for a move – they headed out to a new flat in Bridgeton, just a little further along the River Clyde. 'It was luxury because it had an inside loo,' Lorraine remembers, though she is keen to play down just how bad things had been in her childhood. 'When I told one woman that I had spent the first two years of my life in the Gorbals before moving to Bridgeton, she thought I was talking *Angela's Ashes*. I can assure you it wasn't like that,' she says. 'In reality, it was a very ordinary, working-class environment. We weren't well-off but we were better off than some, and we certainly weren't so poor that we had to eat gravel.'

While Bridgeton was also one of the most disadvantaged areas in the country, Lorraine says it was still a wonderful place to live. 'There were a lot of big families around, the kind who were very, very poor so yes there was a lot of poverty around us. But it was such a great community atmosphere where everyone helped everyone else,' she recalls. It is the kind of spirit that she wishes could be replicated across all of the country today.

The Kelly clan in particular enjoyed nearly a decade of happy, stable years in their flat by the Clyde. Lorraine says her dad was always a grafter, and that she learned her own strong work ethic from his example. By the time she was ready to go to school, he was a fully qualified television repairman, and with ITV establishing itself as a huge rival to the BBC, and *Coronation Street* already becoming a national obsession demand for sets was rising as fast as people's incomes would allow. John worked long hours, aiming to set up his own business and dreaming of a better home even further from the hard heart of Glasgow.

The whole family was in for a shock, though. When Lorraine was six her mother became pregnant again and ultimately gave birth to a happy baby boy, Graham. As the elder sister, Lorraine found she was no longer the centre of her family's universe – and she is happy to admit that she didn't like it. 'It really was a shock to my system and it was certainly strange to have someone else around,' she says. 'I had been the princess until this point. But then along came this beautiful baby boy – and I do mean beautiful. He had blond hair, blue eyes, skin like a peach and he was adorable – people used to stop us in the street just to look at him and ask who he was. I remember him lying on the couch with cushions all around him, enjoying a tiny bottle with a teat on – full of orange juice – and me taking it and drinking it dry.'

That turned out to be just the first of many 'battles' the brother and sister would fight – though both would one day regret all the early tensions that arose between them. 'At first I just treated Graham like a dolly, as any six-year-old girl would. But then I got bored with him. When he got a little older we just didn't get on at all and we fought like cat and dog. I get cross with myself when I think about it because he was a really nice wee guy.'

At the time, though, Lorraine had other things to worry about. The woman who would spend so much of her career talking about weight, diet and body image was getting an early taste of how others saw the subject. 'When I was growing up it was considered really healthy for a child to have chubby cheeks and a fat little body. A sign of good manners was cleaning your plate – and my mum made the best food in the world. Asking for seconds was a sign of being a growing lass – and that was a good thing because I certainly grew. I devoured more than my fair share of pies, cakes and sweeties, as well as my mum's famed mince and potatoes.'

* * * * *

Away from home, however, Lorraine wasn't given an easy time, however. Contemporaries say her first nickname at school was 'Fat Belly Kelly' and she faced some low-level bullying and backchat for another reason as well. 'I got the mickey taken out of me for being a "poshie" because I was always well turned out for school and sometimes got battered because of it,' she remembers. In the afternoons she also went to ballet class and, amazing as it now seems, she remembers herself as being shy and even tongue-tied.

School was still the focus of her life – because her parents had always been focused on education. Anne didn't work while the children were very young and she was determined to prepare them for life's challenges. 'She stayed at home and played with us. She encouraged us in everything, but not in a pushy, hot-house kind of way. I could read and write by the time I was four and I would just eat books from then on,' Lorraine says.

Their grandmother, Margaret McMahon, was equally influential. She had a favourite book that she passed on to the young Lorraine. Called *Van Loon's Lives* and written in 1943, it tells the life stories of great historical figures and describes imaginary dinner parties between them. Lorraine read and re-read it endlessly, finding herself hugely inspired by the stories. And when she was ready to read other things she had plenty of choices. 'Granny had hundreds of books and had instilled a great love of reading and letter-writing in my mother. Mum writes wonderful, mad letters and she then passed that habit on to me,' she says. This love of words would ultimately lead to a passion for news – and to Lorraine's desire to defy her working-class upbringing and become a journalist.

Before then she was also having her eyes opened to the world beyond their tough Glasgow suburb – through the power of television. 'We were one of the first people in our block of flats to ever have a colour television,' Lorraine says, though in truth this was more to do with her father's job than the fact that they had any more money than anyone else. One of the shows she and her dad were often glued to while Anne looked after Graham was *Star Trek* – which first aired in the UK in 1969. Having been given a telescope for her fifth birthday, Lorraine happily admits she had a real daddy's girl and tomboy phase – and while she grew out of that she never lost her love of astronomy and sci-fi. Nearly forty years later her producers on GMTV weren't quite sure if she would pull on a tight, shiny *Star Trek* jumpsuit to film a mock episode with a bunch of die-hard fans. As it turned out she couldn't agree quickly enough.

Another hobby she shared with her dad as a child would also last a lifetime. He took her on a day trip to the Andersonian Museum in Glasgow, where she saw an Emperor penguin egg and started to dream that one day she would visit Antarctica. Again, four decades later she would be ready to jump at the chance to do just that.

* * * * *

When Lorraine was fourteen the Kelly family were finally ready to move again. They headed a few more miles south to East Kilbride, the fast-growing overspill town designed to offer a fresh start to families from Glasgow's inner city. While it never had the cachet of other new towns like Bournville or Welwyn Garden City, it was everything that the Kellys had been hoping to find. 'I had a smashing time living there. We had a lovely, lovely house and I had great pals. It was brilliant,' Lorraine remembers.

Having more space was wonderful – for the first time the family had a house with a garden rather than a tiny flat without even a window box. But Graham says he and his sister still struggled to get along – though he proves that Lorraine had already discovered the gift of the gab that would make her fortune. 'We were always fighting as children and I couldn't really compete because she would talk rings round me. Who watched what on the telly was always a sore point: I'd want to watch cartoons, she'd want *Top Of The Pops*, probably because she was such a big David Bowie fan.'

Hard as it might be to imagine today, Lorraine also had a

year-long phase as a black-clad and gloomy Goth – though she also admits under pressure that 'Maggie May' by Rod Stewart was the first record she bought when she was twelve. The family went to huge efforts to celebrate birthdays with big parties for friends and neighbours, but at Christmas Lorraine and Graham again proved how different they were. 'On Christmas morning we always had a Cadbury Dairy Milk selection and I – greedy pig – would eat the whole box before lunchtime, whereas Graham would have one chocolate and put the rest away. It was the same with pocket money: I would spend it as soon as I got it and he would save it,' she remembers.

But for all the minor battles and differences a near tragedy was about to bring brother and sister closer together. A couple of years later, a second crisis would reinforce this closeness, putting down the foundations for a deep friendship that now shows no sign of ending. The first incident happened just outside the family's new home when Graham was eight and Lorraine fourteen. 'We were all outside playing and Graham just stepped on to the street and this car, speeding, came from nowhere and hit him,' says Lorraine. 'He could have died – he was very seriously injured with a broken leg and internal injuries. It brought it home to me that I really did love him.'

'Lorraine was the first person on the scene to help,' Graham says. 'She was banging on the car bonnet in hysterics because I was half under the car. I was very badly injured and in a state of shock. Lorraine accompanied me to the hospital, where I had to have my spleen removed, and she was so upset because I think she knew how close I had come to being killed.'

The next wake-up call came when Graham was eleven and Lorraine was a self-confessed stroppy teenager on babysitting duty. Graham, who had always suffered from asthma, had one of his biggest attacks to date, forcing Lorraine to phone the doctor's and to try and comfort him until he had been given a nebuliser and an injection of adrenaline to calm the fit. Once more, the crisis made her realise how much she would miss him if he wasn't around – though once again she made sure she didn't show it.

'Graham had pretty good teenage years without too much angst but I went through the usual phase of "hating" everybody, like Harry Enfield's teenage character. But we obviously had strong feelings for one another, which is probably why we used to fight so much. I only started to appreciate how special Graham was when I stopped living in the same house as him. Even if he wasn't my brother I would really like him. I feel lucky to have him, and proud, because he's a decent person.'

Lorraine's other challenge as a teenager was to keep her schoolwork on track at a time when the conditions weren't always ideal. At home, her parents were as keen as ever to see their children get the kind of qualifications that they had themselves missed out on. But Lorraine's school, Claremont High, didn't always make it easy. With about 2,500 pupils it was one of the biggest schools in Scotland at that time, and it didn't have a great reputation back then. 'Claremont was a tough old place – the school magazine had an obituaries page,' jokes former classmate Allan Brown.

Lorraine also suffered some more of the low-level bullying that ultimately made her a whole lot tougher than perhaps she looks. 'I still used to go to school with ringlets and pink ribbons in my hair so I suppose it wasn't really a surprise that I was bullied. But trust me, I was able to stick up for myself,' she says now, with a surprising touch of steel.

Whatever happened in the playground or on the way to school she says she was blessed with some wonderful, dedicated teachers. Her parents were still encouraging her to question everything and had given her a love of learning that would never leave her so she was one of the most enthusiastic pupils in her year.

'I just loved school, I thought it was fantastic. My favourite lesson was English and we had a fantastic teacher called Miss McPhendran and she was real old school. Some of the teachers there were a bit trendy and "Hey, call me Dave," but she was never like that. She had iron-grey hair and you knew there was no way it was ever going to move; it wouldn't have dared. She was big – not fat, sort of Amazonian – and wore a big black cape. She was strict, but you knew where you were with her and I liked that. She was good on the basics and gave us a really good grounding in spelling and grammar, which has stood me in such good stead. She was giving us spelling tests even at the age of thirteen or fourteen – and I still correct the spellings on my scripts to this day.'

* * * * *

Several other people also seemed to thrive on the Claremont High experience in the 1970s. Despite being in an area with huge social problems it seems to have produced far more than its fair share of success stories. Top international hairstylist Alan Edwards was one of them, *Sunday Times* journalist and author Allan Brown another. Then there was *Four Weddings And A Funeral* star John Hannah, a boy who Lorraine took under her wing when she was made house captain. 'In my sixth year I used to take the first years for morning registration. One of them was John Hannah and I still remember exactly where he used to sit. He had this perfect little face and great big dazzling blue eyes. He looked like a wee Furby. He was lovely.'

The other person she remembers plainly from those days is Joyce Woodrow, the former classmate who would end up being her closest lifelong friend. 'We met aged thirteen on a day Lorraine was dressed as a Bay City Roller,' Joyce recalls, to Lorraine's obvious embarrassment. 'But I soon found out that was unusual as Lorraine was more of a David Bowie fan. She was trendy and she loved his records, his style, everything about him.' The other thing Joyce noticed about her new friend was that she was a voracious reader, someone who hated to go anywhere without a book and who spent more in bookshops than she did in record stores.

After becoming firm friends in the classroom, the two were soon ready to venture further afield – on a youth hostelling trip to Edinburgh. 'We were quite naïve in many ways so it was a real adventure,' says Lorraine. 'I remember being terribly jealous of Joyce because she had a rucksack and I thought that was terribly sophisticated.'

Having survived that first trip, Lorraine, Joyce and two other school friends bought Inter Rail cards for a month-long holiday around Europe a couple of years later. As the most methodical and organised of the bunch Lorraine was put in charge of the kitty. She loved it – though the others took a while getting used to her rules. 'We weren't allowed any money to buy biscuits or things like that because Lorraine knew that if we started we would end up blowing the lot,' Joyce says.

Back in East Kilbride the girls were still inseparable. They would sneak nervously into pubs, where Lorraine would have a half of cider and Joyce a half of lager. 'For us, that was really daring,' she says of their so-called teenage rebellion.

However, while she didn't drink much, Lorraine had another vice at sixteen. When her schoolwork got harder she started to eat for Scotland. The puppy fat she had lost over the past few years piled back on with a vengeance. And with typical honesty Lorraine admits she had no one to blame but herself. 'It was getting on towards exam time and I took solace in jumbo-sized packets of crisps and giant chocolate bars.'

Despite this, Graham says his sister never had any trouble finding boyfriends (he remembers her thumping him when he laughed at the first of them and called him a long-haired hippy). For her part Lorraine admits she was never cut out to be a wild child. 'I had my first date at seventeen when I went to the swimming baths with a boy from school and we had a cup of tea afterwards. We went out once or twice after that but I preferred going to the disco in a gang,' she says demurely.

Still, at the age of seventeen, her only major act of rebellion came when her parents went to Greece for a holiday – and it ended in disaster. 'I threw a party while they were away and some gatecrashers did a lot of damage, such as cigarette burns and broken windows. I cleaned up but I knew I had let them down and I still feel guilty about it,' Lorraine says. 'I knew Mum was very disappointed in me. If she had shouted at me I'd have felt better, but she just sort of took one look at the cigarette burns in her new carpet and cried. I felt so small and horrible.'

In a bid to make amends she offered to pay for proper cleaning or even a new carpet. Her parents said no, but by then Lorraine had the kind of work ethic that meant she could have found the money, had she needed to. She got her first

Saturday job just after her fourteenth birthday and was soon collecting £1 a shift working in the Chelsea Girl boutique. After that she moved onwards and upwards, seeing her pay rise up to and beyond the princely sum of 25 pence an hour. And while working at BHS in the city centre she also did a one-day stint at Glasgow's famous Barras market.

'My friend Janice and I got up at 6am one Saturday to bag a pitch. We were selling off bric-a-brac from our mums' houses,' Lorraine says. But at seventeen, she admits, she didn't quite have the confidence to win sales the traditional way. 'In those days the market was full of pitchers doing their stuff with all the amazing patter and we were far too shy to try and shout above those guys. But we sold everything so cheaply that we shifted it all in no time. We went out that night and had a brilliant few days on our profits.'

Back at BHS she was saving up for her first expensive haircut at a trendy Glasgow salon – though she reckons she could have done a better job herself. 'It was the most disastrous haircut of my life, just horrifying. I wanted a fringe but the stylist gave me something short with a huge V at the back. It looked like it came from *Henry V* – in fact, I looked like I was *Henry V*.'

Ultimately, though, Lorraine says her whole childhood could hardly have been better. The girl from the Gorbals thrived on the city's poorest streets. She had been loved all her life; she embraced her education and had her eyes opened to all the possibilities the world had to offer. She says she had also been given the kind of grounding that allows her to cope with all the vastly different people she now meets and all the different experiences she now enjoys.

'Basically I was lucky to have parents who really took the

time and trouble to look after me. They taught me the essential things like saying "please" and "thank you" and respecting others that perhaps we don't have enough of today. And although we were poor my parent always had very high expectations of me as a child, which I then tried to live up to.'

* * * * *

John and Anne's big dream was that their daughter would make it to university – being the first in her family to do so. After only half joking that she wanted to join the RAF and become a fighter pilot, Lorraine had some serious talks with her teachers and picked a tough degree course – she wanted to study English and Russian literature and ultimately become a teacher herself. 'It is the most important job in the world, apart from being a parent, and it makes me furious how undervalued teachers are,' she said, years later. But as her schoolmates started to talk about colleges and courses Lorraine was increasingly distracted. Four years at university sounded wonderful, but she was a girl in a hurry so shouldn't she just go out there now and get a job?

Her love of words, appreciation of history and thirst for knowledge had long since been pushing her in only one direction – journalism. Teaching could wait, she thought. If she couldn't hack it on a newspaper then she could always go back to college later. Suddenly she felt she had to stretch and prove herself. She had big dreams and at just seventeen-years-old Lorraine Kelly was ready to go to work.

2

THE EAST KILBRIDE
NEWS GIRL

'I was probably Glasgow's first yuppie, a real pioneer.'

Finding any job was a real problem in the depressing, strike-torn days of the late 1970s. But finding one in the media was about as tough as you could get. Newspapers are notorious as closed shops, jealously guarding rare vacancies and rejecting the vast majority of applicants. But Lorraine vowed that if a door opened even an inch she would push her way through it. She fired off dozens of letters to editors and applied for journalism courses. She made phone calls, turned up for interviews, wrote endless speculative articles – and with her eighteenth birthday approaching she cracked it. She was offered an internship on the *East Kilbride News* – one of the most sought-after posts in the area. Combining the job with a block release journalism course in Edinburgh meant she worked ridiculously long hours, just as she would for the next five tough years. She would learn her lessons, pay her dues – and she loved it.

Her first beat was typically broad. If it was local, it was

hers. So Lorraine sat through council meetings, wrote up local political scandals, and built up contacts with the fire, police and ambulance services. She reported on local businesses, schools and sports teams; she did the light and frothy stories about charity runs and church fêtes. And she also learned to cope with the grim tasks. While still a teenager herself, she made her first visits to grieving parents of hit-and-run victims; she sat with the families of missing children; in short, she wrote up the seemingly endless series of human tragedies that only local papers ever turn into news.

As the years passed, Lorraine certainly never regretted her decision to go to work rather than stay a student – though she loved hearing the stories of all her old school friends who were living it up in student halls across the country. But she was also in a hurry to leave East Kilbride and buy her own home in Glasgow. She had her eye on a flat right in the city centre long before urban living had come back into vogue. 'I was probably Glasgow's first yuppie, a real pioneer,' she says. The flat was part of one of the city's first regeneration zones, in a development called Hanover Court just behind Queen Street station.

'It was just a wee hutch. When I went to find out more about it the place hadn't even been built so I had to choose it from the plans. I went for one on the third floor and the wee man, in his wee office, pointed upwards and said: "And that'll be your bit of sky," which was so lovely it sold me on it straight away.'

Lorraine was twenty by the time she moved in – and as the brand new property came with everything from carpets to a fitted kitchen she had little else to worry about. 'All I had to do was bring something to sit on, something to watch and something to sleep on. My dad got me a television, of course, I took my bed from my room in East Kilbride and I got myself a £15 sofa.'

Having been able to save only the smallest of deposits, she soon felt the crunch financially. She had spent £20,000 on the flat – a decent amount in 1980 and especially hard to pay for with an almost 100 per cent mortgage. The girl who says she was brought up to fear debt, and never uses a credit card unless she is able to pay off the bill by the end of the month, was watching the pennies from the start. She spent £30 on four chairs and a table from MFI – they were on special offer as they had been dented in the showroom. The one room she didn't pay much attention to was the kitchen – because she took a long time to get to grips with cooking. 'I would occasionally call my mum up and say things like: "I've bought a cabbage, what do I do with it?" My culinary skills consisted of a really good spag bol – and that was it.'

What she remembers most about this time was how much fun it all was. Her neighbours were all young, often hard-up professionals, and Hanover Court was soon nicknamed 'Hangover Court' after a few communal parties too many. 'I remember a group of us being down to our last few pence one night and my best pal, Joyce, taking the money we had clubbed together to buy a bottle of wine, and coming back with something that was non-alcoholic. Twenty years later I still remind her of that,' Lorraine laughs. The lapse was all the more unusual because Joyce was by then building a strong career of her own in pub and club management. One of her jobs was in the John Street Jam pub, as it was called then, where Lorraine would rush for a stiff drink after a tough day at the paper.

On the *East Kilbride News* Lorraine had been impressing her editors for several years. She is remembered as one of the keenest and hardest working of the cub reporters they took on in that era – and was the only one to be offered the chance to write regular comment pieces as well as news stories. Ultimately, she ended up being given her own page for hard-hitting opinion pieces – one of her first being about drink-driving after yet another local tragedy had hit the headlines. 'I don't like the fuzziness around the law and I feel very strongly about it,' she argued, making her comments both personal and controversial. 'Don't allow one or two drinks. Ban it completely. If I'm driving I won't even have half a glass of wine.'

The promotion to columnist was great for her career, but it was lousy for her social life. 'When I did go out I used to go to gay clubs in Glasgow because the music was brilliant and the dancing was fantastic, but I wasn't a big clubber. I couldn't be, because I always worked. I always had an early morning to be ready for the next day.'

And she had other challenges as well. She was relentlessly self-improving, and joined the Junior Chamber of Commerce to try and learn new skills and meet inspiring new people. On top of this, Lorraine was finding herself affected by many of the stories she covered at the paper. Her parents had given her a profound social conscience and a sense that you should always do what you can to help others and so she would squeeze extra hours out of her days to try and do just that.

'One day I was doing a story about some work that the British Heart Foundation had done locally and I was so moved by it that I decided to do some fund-raising after hours. I organised discos and jumble sales, took some pensioners on a day out to the seaside and even roller-skated from East Kilbride to Edinburgh to raise sponsorship money.'

In the process, Lorraine earned an unexpected reward – the charity was offering a prize draw for the person who raised money in the most ridiculous ways. That person turned out to be Lorraine. She was given tickets for two to Rio de Janeiro, Brasil, and she took her mum Anne with her. While there, she learned another lesson about life that would never leave her. 'It was a great trip,' she says, 'but I was uneasy about the fact that from one side of our hotel you could see the Copacabana beach where the girls were stunning and there was a huge amount of money. On the other side there were poor folk living under corrugated iron. I couldn't really get my head around that.'

* * * * *

Back in Scotland again, Lorraine began to wonder if she had been at the *East Kilbride News* for too long. Always a girl with a plan – and a girl in a hurry – she was getting itchy feet and had a new challenge in mind. She felt she had proved herself as a print journalist, but could she do as well researching and writing for a television station? The BBC seemed the obvious place to find out and its staff soon started to get used to Lorraine's calls. 'I used to pester them and phone them all the time,' she says. 'I started by putting myself up for the role of farming correspondent, which I didn't get, and then applied for absolutely every job there I ever saw advertised.' She also called up constantly to see if there might be any other jobs on offer just to those in the know. Fortunately, when something did come up, they remembered her name.

The job in question was as a lowly researcher at BBC Scotland – and while Lorraine's wage at the newspaper had been pretty lousy, this one was even worse. She accepted the job and took a £2,000-a-year pay cut, and could no longer afford her mortgage repayments. But, as ever, she had a plan.

Just around the corner from 'Hangover Court' was a diner called Charlie Parkers. Waitresses there earned a basic wage of £1 an hour and otherwise depended on tips. Lorraine thought she could defy expectations and balance her books by working there. 'It was really quite a glamorous place and I am not at all glamorous,' she remembers, with a sigh. 'But I was the comedy turn. I used to get great tips because I would make people laugh. And I think the manager only kept me on because I made him laugh as well.' The uniform was only one of the stumbling blocks she had to try to overcome. 'We all had to wear high heels and shorts and the problem was that all the other girls were more like supermodels, all slim with great long legs. Then I would roll up, dishevelled and tired from a full day at work, refusing to tuck my shirt into my shorts because I felt like a little tub.' But it wasn't just the look that Lorraine got wrong back then. 'Once I tried to make this poor customer an Irish coffee but the only way I could get the cream to float was by shoving in loads of sugar. The guy took one sip and nearly threw up.'

She is keen to point out that she wasn't the only bad waitress in the city in those days – she reckons her old pal Joyce was also vying for the honour. Joyce was working at a trendy place called The Spaghetti Factory and one night Lorraine, along with a new boy she had just started seeing, decided to drop in on her. 'We both ordered spaghetti Bolognese. Joyce was desperate to make a good impression but unfortunately as she was bringing over the Parmesan cheese she slipped and it all ended up going in my open handbag on the floor.'

On a more serious note, Lorraine admits that having two jobs was leaving her exhausted. It was really hard, working until the early hours after a full day's work at the BBC, but she was brought up to believe that bills have to be paid and that you work whatever hours you need to work to pay them.

'I'm a pit pony when it comes to work and I learned to be one right from the start. I started work at 14. As a child it was all: "What do you mean you've got a broken leg and an iron lung? Get to school!" Yes, the hours were long, but I'd have noticed them more if I was down a mine. My parents instilled the working-class work ethic into me from the start, that real Calvinistic thing. You never skip school, you turn up on time, you work your shift, you never skive, you respect money but you aren't obsessed by it.'

That said, a little more money wouldn't have gone amiss for Lorraine in the early 1980s. During her quiet moments at Charlie Parkers, she would stand by the door and look longingly at the Rogano restaurant on the Royal Exchange Square, which had the reputation of attracting the rich and famous and, back then, had a really strict door policy. 'Liz Taylor had dined there and apparently even Ted Heath was turned away when he was Prime Minister because he hadn't booked a table. I could never have afforded to go there back then, but I always hoped that one day I might be able to make it happen.'

Meanwhile, Lorraine was starting to worry that leaving newspapers for the BBC had been a bad move. Every day, she commuted on the 'clockwork orange' – the city's fifteen-station circular underground network – but she got none of the buzz she had experienced on the *East Kilbride News*. 'The experience was really valuable but it was pretty miserable at the BBC,' she remembers.

Like most of her fellow researchers she was hoping that one day she might get out of the back office and on to the screen, though for her the desire had been a long time coming. 'I always used to joke that the only thing I knew about television was that my dad fixed them for a living,' she says. Her great aunt had been a dancer with the Scottish equivalent of the Tiller Girls but Lorraine had never wanted to follow in her footsteps and go on stage. She had never been in any school plays or joined the local drama group, so could she suddenly break out of her shell and shine in front of the cameras?

But the more she thought about it, the more Lorraine wanted to give it a try. It was another big challenge for someone who was already making a habit of climbing mountains. In a pattern that would soon be her hallmark, it turned out that the more people who told her she would never make it, the more determined she became to prove them wrong. The big problem, however, was an unwritten rule that you had to speak with the BBC's standard 'received pronunciation', or maybe a posh Edinburgh accent, before you were allowed on screen. Lorraine had neither – but she still managed to get a camera crew together and head out on to the streets one day to help film some vox pops with members of the public. If it went well, she thought, it would be her calling card to more on-screen jobs in the future. And, as she worked on the footage in the editing suite, she genuinely thought the segment had been a success.

'Lorraine, can you come in and see me for a moment?'

When she got the call from the chief producer later that day she was convinced he must agree. But she couldn't have been more wrong. She was going to get the shock of her life.

'I sat down in his office and he said: "We can't have you on television. Your accent is no good." He said it was too Glaswegian, he even used the word "offensive" to describe it. Finally, he told me I would have to have elocution lessons before I was ever to go on screen again. It was a huge shock, it was crazy.'

Shell-shocked and angry Lorraine headed back to her desk to stew. Away from the office she talked about the rejection with friends. Should she give up her new dreams and put up with a life in the broadcasting backroom? Should she find an elocution teacher and change the way she was to try and succeed? Or should she simply rise above all this and make a success of her life on her own terms? None of her colleagues were surprised when their tough little friend took the latter option. She had decided that her boss would be the latest person she would prove wrong – and she would never regret it.

'Ultimately this turned out to be the best thing the guy could have done for me, because my ultimate reaction was just "Bugger you". It really offended me and I thought, no way, I'll show you, and it was a huge spur for me to move on and ultimately up.'

Fortunately for Lorraine, the BBC wasn't the only television channel in Glasgow in the 1980s. The brash new breakfast-time station TV-am had an office there as well, and Lorraine decided that if she was going to get a job there she might as well take her request right to the top. Using the confidence she had gained as a newspaper reporter she picked up the phone and asked to be put through to the controversial new editor-in-chief of TV-am, Greg Dyke. Amazingly, he took the call and she asked the famously abrasive executive for a job in his Glasgow studio. He found her one.

'The balls of me! I can't imagine being able to do that,' she says now when she thinks back. She also couldn't quite believe how big a gamble she was taking by refusing to accept the status quo at the BBC – because a tiny bit of her had to accept that when it came to accents her BBC boss had been right. 'Back then no one on the telly talked like me. No one had strong regional accents at that point. But I just had a feeling that this had to change.' She was right, not least because Aussie Bruce Gyngell, the new boss at TV-am, was thinking exactly the same. After several secret meetings, interviews and screen tests Lorraine was offered a new contract at TV-am. Little more than nine months after starting at the BBC she handed in her resignation and prepared for her fresh challenge.

At her leaving party, Lorraine's former colleagues crowded around and gossiped about the industry. There were mixed opinions about whether she was doing the right thing. Some pointed to the huge financial and ratings crisis that had engulfed TV-am since it started broadcasting little more than a year earlier. At the start it was led by media heavyweights David Frost, Angela Rippon, Anna Ford and Michael Parkinson. They had been given a 'mission to explain' – but audiences didn't want to know. Within months the station was losing huge sums of money, triggering rows and resignations backstage and in the boardroom. The BBC's *Breakfast Time* show, by contrast, was booming.

So was Lorraine backing the wrong horse by quitting the Beeb and joining TV-am? While no one could predict the future, Lorraine was convinced she was doing the right thing.

She had enjoyed talking to Greg Dyke when she had called up, incensed at the BBC and practically demanding a job from him. She had got a taste of his enthusiasm and energy, of his determination to shake up the channel. And as a viewer she was convinced TV-am had already turned a corner. The friendly faces of Anne Diamond and Nick Owen were now on the sofa for the flagship morning show (as well as the puppet Roland Rat, jokingly referred to by insiders as 'the only rat to ever join a sinking ship'). Ratings were edging up and the staff Lorraine met in her first few days on the station were equally optimistic. There was a near palpable sense that TV-am was a place of opportunity, that everything was possible for those who worked hard. And with hard work firmly in her DNA, Lorraine could hardly have felt more at home.

Her job title, in the autumn of 1984, was Scottish correspondent. This meant she had to cover any and every story the producers and news desk threw at her. From the start, she was on call and could be bleeped twenty-four hours a day, seven days a week, and she was – darting off to report back on fires and floods, road accidents and riots, crime scenes and crack houses. It was a steep learning curve and an adrenaline-filled thrill from day one.

'I always had a bag packed with clean knickers, a toothbrush and extra socks so that I was ready to head out for a story even in the middle of the night – which happened a lot more often than you might think. As part of the TV-am team we covered everything, went everywhere. Not only news but sport, features, music, quirky human stories, everything.'

Her parents say they were amazed at the transformation in their daughter. 'Seeing her on television was just extraordinary, and even if I had to get up at 6am I would sit and watch the whole programme,' recalls Anne. 'We were so proud of her when she was the *East Kilbride* news girl, and we've been proud of her ever since she went on television.'

In 1984, though, Anne and John were also a little bit shocked at the new confidence their daughter was displaying. 'When John and I heard Lorraine talking shop to the producers about the next day's show, for example, we were really impressed because she sounded so professional. For my part I am just amazed at Lorraine's ambition and I don't know where she gets it from,' says Anne.

Others were starting to recognise it as well, and Lorraine was winning some influential supporters. 'I've often turned on the television at some godforsaken hour and seen Lorraine at some disaster or other, standing in the snow or the rain. There are no excuses from Lorraine. She's always been someone who gets out there and does the job and that's why she's a good reporter rather than just another pretty face,' said Hugh Terris, one of her former journalism lecturers, of his erstwhile charge. 'She may be sweet but Lorraine is very direct and very sure of what she wants,' remarked Scotland's *Daily Record* reporter Roz Paterson after first meeting the woman who was fast becoming one of the most recognisable faces in Scotland.

Back then, after little more than a year in her new job, Lorraine says ambition and excitement carried her through – and her desire to succeed meant she was constantly asking her producers to find her new stories to cover, wherever and whenever they might be. But while her mum and best friend Joyce say they could tell that she was thriving, Lorraine admitted that the role did take a heavy toll on her personal life and even her health: 'It was physically and emotionally hard. I had no social life and I could never get blootered. And being on call twenty-four hours a day meant I would just grab food whenever I could – takeaways, microwave meals, bags of crisps. There was dust on my cooker for years.'

Fortunately, the TV-am crew that she tended to work with were good company. 'Ambitious but not ruthless,' was how one of her first producers described their on-camera talent. Others applauded the fact that Lorraine was always happy to muck in with the rest of them – and was never shy of buying a round of drinks when the cameras were off. So while she had split up with her boyfriend in her first year at TV-am – mainly because she was either away or too tired to spend time with him – she didn't feel short of friends. After a while, one of those new friends was to become much more. Lorraine was starting to fall for her cameraman, Steve Smith, and their relationship was to move up a gear one long night in Glencoe.

The pair were filming a story about the mountain rescue teams, with Lorraine taking on the part of a victim dumped high up the mountain in a snowdrift. 'It was a giggle, and later on we were having a few drinks in the bar when we looked at each other and, suddenly, something clicked,' she remembers. 'Because we had worked together for about a year and got on brilliantly as friends, I always say it was friendship at first sight. And it was all the better for that.'

For his part, Steve reckons he could have blown his chances by coming up with what the couple still jokingly refer to as the least likely chat-up line in history. 'Do you fancy coming to see Dundee United play Hearts?' he asked at the bar that night. Fortunately Lorraine said 'Yes' without missing a beat. And so the following weekend they wrapped up warm, headed off to Tannadice Park and sat through one of the dullest draws of the season.

'Steve was mortified because he thought I would never want to see him or United again,' Lorraine says. 'But I was hooked on them both – I had found the whole day really romantic and I'd really enjoyed everything about the game.' And so the girl whose father had taken her to Rangers' games more than a decade earlier got ready to switch her allegiance. Lorraine knows far more about football than many people might expect. She remembers well all the big names at Rangers, including the likes of Derek Johnstone and Derek Parlane, who played in the first games she watched. And years later, she still harks back to the glory days at Dundee. 'United played brilliant football back in the 1980s. They had the likes of David Narey, Paul Hegarty and Paul Sturrock when he was still skinny and beautiful. Virtually every single player in that United team had come up through the ranks and was so committed. That's what attracted me to the team after Steve had taken me there for the first time and turned me into a lifelong fan.'

For the next twenty-five years and beyond, Lorraine would follow Dundee United's fortunes – calling herself an 'eternal optimist' in the bad times and even ringing up local radio stations in the town to offer her advice on the latest club crisis. She also raised some eyebrows when she said she always wore her favourite 'lucky tartan knickers' when the team was playing key games – even if she was miles away in England or overseas at the time.

Lorraine and Steve's next big date in 1985 was a little bit more romantic than an evening on the terraces at Tannadice. They were both in line for a rare weekend off, so they decided to head west to Mull where they found a tiny, isolated hotel. 'We went for a long walk and got drenched. But later we ate

Mull cheese on homemade oatcakes and drank a cracking bottle of red wine in bed. It was fab,' she remembers.

Back at work and back on call the pair decided they should move in together, and started a gypsy existence that would characterise and cement their relationship for the next five years. 'I still had my tiny rabbit hutch of a flat in Glasgow, about ten minutes from the studio, so we lived there during the week and then we moved into Steve's flat in Dundee at weekends,' Lorraine says. A clever division of labour provided instant domestic bliss: having survived on beans on toast as a single girl she was more than happy to let Steve cook meat, two veg and all the trimmings every night now they were a couple. 'Basically, I was happy to let Steve do the cooking while I opened the wine,' she says. 'He can cook a curry to die for while I can open the wine faster than anyone I know. So we made a good team.'

After their first, blissful weekend away together in Mull, the couple's joint holidays were not always to prove so successful, however. Desperate to escape the Scottish winter, but both still utterly broke, the most they could afford for their first big trip was a week in Tunisia – in January. It was the lowest of the low season and while the hotel looked idyllic in the brochure, basically it was still being built. There was scaffolding up one side of it and the sound of drilling was deafening. To make matters worse, it was in the middle of nowhere, there were no shops or even a beach nearby. 'Then we saw our room and it looked like a prison cell with two single beds, a tiny window and not enough room to swing a bikini. It was cloudy and wet when we arrived, the bad weather didn't lift and it took ages to trek to the nearest town. We spent a lot of time hungry.'

With hindsight, the pair say it might have been better if they had stayed this way – because when they did start eating things got even worse. 'After one very bad meal we both got terrible food poisoning and were quite literally fighting over the bathroom for the next three days,' Lorraine says of the Tunisian experience.

Relationship experts say these kinds of disasters can either force couples apart or tie them even closer together. For Lorraine and Steve it was the latter. 'The whole holiday was utterly miserable and probably the most unromantic experience imaginable but I did think that if we still loved each other after that we could survive anything,' says Lorraine.

As it turned out, the trip would set the tone for almost all of the pair's future holidays. 'It seems as if every time we go away together we end up in casualty,' Lorraine says. The following year, for example, the pair had a bit more cash to spend and flew out to stay in some beach huts in Thailand. Steve hit his head on a boat and needed medical treatment – and while some sympathy from Lorraine might have been in order he wasn't going to get it. 'He came out of hospital after having stitches and I burst out laughing. They had bandaged his head and tied the spare bandage into a bow so it looked as if he had these huge, stupid ears like Mickey Mouse. It was hysterical – or at least it was to me,' she remembers.

Back at work, their love affair started to give them a surprising career boost. For some time the TV-am bosses had been praising Lorraine and her crew not just for being ready to cover any story, anywhere, but for almost always beating the rival stations and being first on the scene. Lorraine decided it was only fair to explain why this was. 'While other crews were trying to track down their cameraman, I had mine tucked up in bed with me,' she joked to colleagues.

* * * * *

While so much was going well in her life and her career, Lorraine did have one worry as she approached her mid-twenties. She was finding it harder to ignore the fact that she needed glasses. 'My mum, dad and brother all wore them and for years I thought I had escaped. But the television screens were getting more blurred and I had to do something about it,' she said. Armed with a prescription she set out to choose her first pair – and made an immediate fashion error. 'I decided that if I had to have glasses then I might as well go for ones with enormous frames. They were just a bog standard price, nothing posh, but they were massive. I thought they were so fashionable but I basically looked like the Fearless Fly.'

Unfortunately, this turned out to be only half the problem. Because she wasn't used to having glasses, she kept sitting on them, dropping them and treading on them. 'In the end I had to keep them together with sticking plaster and was going around looking like *Coronation Street*'s Jack Duckworth. I couldn't possibly wear them on screen so just before I was due to do a report I used to whip them off and hand them to the cameraman.'

But in a moment worthy of her comedy favourite, Lucille Ball, Lorraine admits that things didn't always go this smoothly. 'My job back then really wasn't glamorous, whatever it might have looked like on screen. One time we were halfway up a mountain in the freezing cold, doing an early morning report and I had hurt my neck so I was wearing a surgical collar and three coats to keep warm. I handed the cameraman two of the coats, then the surgical collar but almost forgot my Jack Duckworth glasses.'

Her cameraman that morning – as he was most mornings – was Steve. Because he was so used to seeing his girlfriend in her Fearless Fly glasses, he nearly forgot about them as well, but at the last moment he remembered. Lorraine handed them over and viewers were spared what both said would not have been a pretty sight over breakfast.

Being able to laugh about incidents like this made the pair's professional and personal relationship even stronger. Best pal Joyce says it was clear that this was a love affair built to last – even though a few sudden separations were to put it to an unexpected test.

The first split came in 1987, when Lorraine spent two months in America as part of a major leap up the career ladder. TV-am was grooming her for a bigger role and wanted to see if she had what it took to cover news, human interest, entertainment and political stories from overseas. She spent half her posting in Los Angeles, half in Washington DC, and unwittingly proved herself to be more serious about her job than many of her new American colleagues.

'I was doing a piece at the White House, a serious news piece about American politics, and they asked if I could run through it all again. The American cameraman was really concerned about the first version so I was worried that maybe I hadn't got my head around the politics or hadn't said it well enough. But it was nothing like that. He was just worried that my hair looked a bit messy. Now I don't care how many hairs I have out of place as long as it's not distracting to viewers, but in the States they seemed more interested in the way that I looked than in what I was saying.'

Shortly after coming back to Scotland and back on permanent call for TV-am, Lorraine was sent back to the airport. She was flown out to New York for one of the station's flagship celebrity interviews, this time with Annie Lennox at the height of her Eurhythmics fame. What the two women couldn't believe, after the interview was in the can, was that neither of them had needed to be in the USA after all. 'Annie had been in Aberdeen, where she was living back then, and I had been in Dundee. Neither of us could believe they had flown us thousands of miles for the interview when we had started out just a few miles down the road from each other. Not that we were complaining, of course.'

Lorraine's next two flights illuminated both the serious and the exciting sides of her job. The first was when she climbed nervously into a helicopter before dawn one morning to fly out to cover the story of another helicopter's fatal crash. The second, shortly afterwards, came when she pulled on a G-suit to do an interview in a Hunter jet being flown – sometimes upside down – through the valleys and over the lochs of the Highlands. It was exhilarating stuff and it looked as if a whole lot more was on the cards.

* * * * *

TV-am bosses sent Lorraine to the company doctor for cholera, polio, yellow fever and tetanus jabs. After her successes in LA, Washington and New York they were ready to give her a roving international role, adding her to their roster of proven, reliable reporters who could cover any story, in any part of the world and at any time. But as it turned out the jabs were hardly needed. Because in 1987 and 1988 all the big news stories of the moment seemed to happen in Scotland. TV-am wanted Lorraine first on the spot to cover each of them.

The first flared up in October 1987 when rioting erupted at Peterhead Prison in the north east of the country. Around 50 of the jail's most dangerous prisoners took control of the infamous D Block and the SAS was ultimately sent in to break up the siege. Similar mini riots broke out across the country over the next few months, with Lorraine reporting live on almost all of them.

On 6 July 1988, however, an even bigger story broke. Just before 10pm a series of explosions were reported some 120 miles off the north-east coast of Scotland. The Piper Alpha oil rig was ablaze, with smoke and flames soaring 350 feet into the night sky. A huge rescue operation was launched, with around 30 helicopters and boats heading out to what was the largest and oldest oil platform in the North Sea.

Early reports said some 225 men were working on the Occidental Oil rig, and when Lorraine and her crew arrived in Aberdeen in time for the live broadcasts the following morning it seemed that precious few had been brought back alive. The first interviews she carried out were with the coastguard and emergency service staff who were co-ordinating the rescue. She followed this by speaking to the oil bosses and engineers who described the structure itself and its likely condition after such a fierce explosion. Then, most memorably, came the families of the missing workers, the hospital staff who were helping survivors, and the bereaved.

Lorraine remained in Aberdeen for three weeks that summer, broadcasting every day in the aftermath of what was the worst North Sea oil disaster ever seen. Along with other reporters, such as the BBC's Mike Donkin, Lorraine and her crew did take risks. Four days after the explosion, for example, she was called to a helicopter launch pad at 4.30am for a safety briefing before being flown out to sea and past the smouldering rig itself. They landed on Texaco's Tartan platform, the closest to Piper Alpha, the first reporters to have got this close to the scene of the tragedy and the first to fly past it. After four hours on Tartan, filming and interviewing the workers there, they flew back over the North Sea to Aberdeen.

'There was total silence in the helicopter as we passed Piper Alpha,' said the Texaco director of the tense journey. By then the scale of the disaster had become more apparent. A total of 59 people were brought back alive from the rig – but 167 were not. The town of Aberdeen was in shock and mourning, and Lorraine continued to be in the middle of the debate as everyone tried to piece together exactly what had happened and how it could be prevented from ever occurring again.

Heading back to Glasgow in August 1998, Lorraine was mentally and physically exhausted, but more was to come: 'I thought the Piper Alpha catastrophe was the worst human tragedy I would ever see, that I would never again tackle anything as awful. Then, of course, in the winter came Lockerbie.'

3

LIVE FROM LOCKERBIE

*I always knew that however awful I felt I was only reporting on it.
I wasn't living it like all those poor souls had to. I could walk away
and I always remembered that they couldn't.'*

The first indications of the awful tragedy came in the evening of 21 December 1988. Christmas was in the air. But it was soon to be forgotten.

Pan Am Flight 103 had taken off as normal from London Heathrow, bound for New York with 259 passengers and crew on board – including three children. Just after 7pm, the plane disappeared off the radar screens. It had been travelling at 31,000 feet when a bomb went off, after being smuggled on board by two Libyan terrorists. Everyone on board died instantly, along with 11 residents of the small town of Lockerbie that lay under the flight path. Debris from the explosion was to spread over nearly 900 square miles.

It was an event Lorraine says she will never forget. 'We were there three-quarters of an hour after it happened. The A74 had burnt-out cars all over it. The only thing that kept me going at first was that it was so dark that you couldn't really see what was happening. The smell of burning aircraft fuel, the smoke in the air, it was hellish. There were loads of ambulances, but they didn't have anything to do because everyone was dead. So many people were dead.' Her voice tails off as she remembers the sights she and the crew saw, and the people they spoke to in those first harrowing hours after the explosion.

What made the event even more important for Lorraine and the TV-am crew was that the likes of Sky News and BBC News 24 were still to be launched. So the breakfast crews were the only rolling news providers on the scene. When Lorraine and colleagues such as Martin Frizzell went live on ITV on the morning of 22 December, millions of shocked viewers were watching them, and their first three-and-a-half-hour broadcast was one of the most important that the channel had ever made.

Lorraine remembers being in local residents' homes and businesses. She recalls walking through the chaos and the darkness of the first awful night, trying to bring a sense of perspective to it the following morning. In common with most of the other reporters there, she says the whole scene frequently seemed unreal. But the stories of those who had lost relatives and friends were not. Neither were the hugs Lorraine gave people after the cameras had stopped rolling. What made the story harder for everyone in the borders was, of course, that Christmas was approaching, though it hardly felt like it.

'Everybody was taking down their Christmas decorations. What was there to celebrate? I was there on Christmas Day, filing reports like all the other days as the tragedy all carried on unfolding,' Lorraine remembers. And away from the cameras she needed somewhere private to break down. She found it with her parents. 'My dad picked me up one day to take me home and I just poured it all out to him in the car and then at home. My way of coping was to pour it all out to my family.'

To her credit, she tried to ensure that her own feelings never overshadowed those of all the distraught relatives she met, either at Lockerbie, Piper Alpha or any of the other tragedies she has reported on over the years. 'I always knew that however awful I felt, I was only reporting on it,' she says of Lockerbie in particular. 'I wasn't living it, like all those poor souls had to do. I could walk away, and I always remembered that they couldn't. It wasn't just a story to them, and that's something all journalists should bear in mind, but sometimes forget to do.'

* * * * *

As 1989 got underway, Lorraine was no longer just splitting her time between her flat in Glasgow and Steve's home in Dundee. London was calling and she was spending increasing amounts of time south of the border as well. At this point TV-am's iconic studios in Camden, north London were almost as famous as the breakfast programmes themselves. Converted from an old garage and designed by architect Terry Farrell, the most famous design element was the huge plastic egg-cups on the roof, which are still there today above the faint outlines of the old TV-am logo.

For Lorraine, though, the building tended to be shrouded in darkness when she arrived for her first few weeks of studio-based trial runs. She was on early, first filling in on *The Morning Programme* and then guest-presenting *Summer Sunday* and *Frost On Sunday* when the usual hosts were on holiday. The host of the final show, none other than David Frost himself, left particularly big shoes to fill. But the TV-am bosses felt Lorraine was more than up to the task, and they were prepared to give her plenty of room to grow.

'I think I had come to the bosses' notice because I had been reporting for them almost every day for the past year. Doing the 6am to 7am slots was great because I was able to make all my mistakes there,' Lorraine remembers of her early London-based shows. 'Nobody shouted from the rooftops that I was going to become the next big thing in breakfast television so I was just allowed to get on with my job and learn my craft.'

With typical honesty, Lorraine is the first to admit that she had plenty to learn. Presenting and controlling a show from a studio was a completely different job to reporting on news or other events out in the field. Television insiders say it requires a totally different style, pace and set of skills. At first, she says, she simply didn't have them. 'When I look back on my performance then I cringe,' she says, years later. 'I was young, raw, inexperienced and I spoke too quickly and used too many colloquialisms which simply weren't right for that environment.'

What the bosses liked about Lorraine was that she was prepared to take criticism on board and was always ready to try and improve her performance. They say it was also clear that she was on top of the news and current affairs agenda and was able to convey some of the most complex political issues in a way that every viewer could understand. After a while, it became apparent that the gamble of bringing this Scottish livewire down to England appeared to have paid off. From then on, Lorraine's one- and two-week stints in the London studio would become a lot more regular and start to last much longer. She became a regular resident of the TV-am flat in west London. And while she didn't know it, she was being groomed for one of the biggest roles in British television.

4

GOOD MORNING
BRITAIN

'Big shoulder pads, big buttons, earrings like plates!
And my hair – it looked like a giant helmet had been
lowered on to my head by a crane.'

B y the end of the 1980s, the best seat in the broadcasting
house was on the main sofa at TV-am. Viewing figures
had soared from a low of just 100,000 in 1983 to more than
1.8 million at the end of the decade. The flagship show, *Good
Morning Britain,* was becoming a national institution and
had made huge stars out of co-hosts Anne Diamond and Nick
Owen. But by the time Lorraine arrived in London things
were changing fast.

Nick had left to join ITV Sport in 1986 and Anne had since
shared the sofa with the likes of Mike Morris, Richard Keys,
Geoff Meade and David Foster. She was still the nation's
favourite presenter, but the easy chemistry she had enjoyed
with Nick was hard to recover and it was hard to ignore the
rumours that she too was ready for a change.

Lorraine was back with Steve in Glasgow when the news
broke that Anne was indeed quitting the sofa and creating
the most sought-after vacancy in television. Looking back it

is hard to remember quite why this story was deemed to be so important, or just how big a deal the TV-am job was. But as Lorraine and her colleagues digested the information, the newspapers were moving into overdrive. Acres of newsprint were devoted to the departure and to the question of Anne's replacement. 'It is the quest for a flawless diamond', was how one paper put it. 'In that twentieth-century religion called television, the quest is being compared to the search for the Holy Grail: Just who can replace Anne Diamond at TV-am?'

* * * * *

Despite never thinking of herself as a full-time, studio-based presenter rather than an on-the-road reporter Lorraine was suddenly being tipped for the top. But she wasn't alone. A battalion of ambitious presenters was also lining up in the wings. Existing TV-am players including Ulrika Jonsson, Caroline Righton, Jayne Irving, Kathy Tayler, Kay Burley, Trish Williamson and Kathy Rochford, were all in the frame for promotion. But by the autumn of 1989, the field had been narrowed down to just two key players. And as Lorraine was invited back down south for her own test run on the *Good Morning Britain* sofa, the Welsh reporter Linda Mitchell was heading east. TV-am bosses had decided to put the pair together for a breakfast-time *Pop Idol*-style face-off. Lorraine and Linda both had the chance to sit alongside Mike Morris and Richard Keys as guest presenters on the show and viewers were asked to vote on the one they liked the most.

At first Lorraine's odds of winning looked long. The TV-am

switchboard was deluged with complaints about her accent and dozens of viewers wrote in saying they couldn't understand a word the new presenter was saying. Broadcasting insiders sapped her confidence still further by saying she simply didn't have the look that channel bosses Bruce Gyngell and Greg Dyke were hoping for. 'Officially speaking, what Bruce Gyngell wants is an experienced journalist who is relaxed and informal in front of the camera, bright and cheerful first thing in the morning, and who can get the news across while still doing all the showbiz interviews,' said a fellow executive. 'Unofficially we all know that to be one of Gyngell's girls you also have to be young, stunning, suntanned and look pretty in pink.'

Lorraine knew her journalistic training meant she could meet the first half of the criteria. But did she really want to win a job by virtue of looking pretty in pink? The *Daily Mail* inadvertently raised her old insecurities as the selection process dragged on. In its analysis of the two key candidates for the job it said Lorraine had the looks 'of a classic forties film star' – not a description that fitted the modern, youthful image that TV-am was trying to project.

But for all the doubts and internal criticisms Lorraine turned out to be the viewers' choice – something that wouldn't change for the next twenty years. She won the full-time slot next to Mike Morris. And while she is proud to say she hardly ever wore pink, she admits that the clothes she did choose have hardly stood the test of time. In 2006, for example, she was a guest on *Friday Night With Jonathan Ross* when he flashed a huge photo on to the screen showing her on her first day in the big new role. She shrieked with embarrassment. 'Look at me! It's all big shoulder pads, big buttons, earrings like plates. And my hair! It looks like a giant helmet had been lowered on to my head by a crane! Get that off the screen!'

Looks apart, Lorraine fell in love with the whole *Good Morning Britain* routine. From Monday to Friday she lived in the TV-am flat in Notting Hill, rising just after 3.30am every morning and arriving at the north London studios just before 5. It was a gruelling schedule, but she says it was far less stressful than her on-call days in Scotland when she could be paged at any hour of the day or night and told to cross Scotland for a story at a moment's notice.

The sheer variety of the magazine-style show was also perfect for her skills and her personality. 'I'm a terrible gab – with me I go from: "What's going on in Yugoslavia?" to "Did you see *Coronation Street* last night?" in a heartbeat, and I'm passionate about them both,' she told reporters who asked how she was getting on after she passed her six-month anniversary. '*Good Morning Britain* helps me keep in touch with absolutely everything that's going on, from hard news to some really fun features.'

She and Mike were equally happy with each other, bouncing ideas and comments around before, during and after their shows and making many viewers forget that Anne and Nick had ever existed. For Lorraine, it was all just like a totally unexpected dream come true.

'I was quite happy in Scotland and just toddled down to London to do a few reporting shifts and all of a sudden I ended up doing the main programme,' is how she describes it, with typical modesty. 'I've never had a career plan or sat down and said to myself: "Where will I be in five years' time?" and I certainly didn't do that when I started at TV-am. My big worry about goals like that is what you do if you are disappointed? Anyway, five-year plans and the like remind me of Stalin and that's not how I want my life to be. If everything stopped tomorrow it wouldn't worry me. There are more important things than your work.'

If pressed, Lorraine admits that the most important element of her life back then was Steve. But for all her smiles on camera she told friends that her move to London had put their relationship under severe pressure. 'Our relationship had begun with us seeing each other 24 hours a day, seven days a week for about a year and a half. We then went from living in each other's pockets to hardly seeing one another. We speak every day and he sees me on television so he knows I'm OK, but it's obviously not the same. Anyone who has had a long-distance relationship knows how difficult this can be.'

Fortunately, the big pay rise Lorraine had earned when she got the *Good Morning Britain* contract meant she could afford to fly back to Dundee to see Steve every weekend. But even this didn't always seem to smooth out the new wrinkles in their relationship. 'I would get home on Friday evening and it would take a few hours to get back to normal. We would dance around each other not wanting to argue about anything because our time together was so precious. Then, by the time we got back to normal it was Sunday and time for me to come back down to London. It was hard and the commuting was exhausting but it never crossed my mind to do anything differently because the relationship was so important to me,' she says.

She also says it never crossed her mind to worry if Steve was being faithful to her in Scotland – and when one of her TV-am colleagues once asked her if she trusted him she offered just one word in reply: Implicitly.

As it turned out, Steve wasn't the only person north of the border to be worrying about how Lorraine was coping on her own. Her mother, Anne, was equally concerned. 'I used to ring her at night to check she had locked her front door,' she says with a smile. 'I'd worry terribly that she was walking home at night on her own or that she wasn't looking after herself properly.'

Anne would also do what she had done from the very start of her daughter's television career: She got up early to watch every moment of Lorraine's screen time. In the process she spotted just how quickly her daughter had got to grips with what the industry calls 'sofa-style'. 'We speak on the phone almost every day and I tell her sometimes: "You were butting in" or "You let that man ramble on too long," but that's very rare because she is great at her job.' Viewers agreed. Lorraine turned out to be just the kind of person the country wanted to wake up to. She could inform and explain when required. She could laugh and talk away when technical hitches off screen meant airtime had to be filled. Most importantly, she was entirely in tune with the vast majority of her viewers.

'At the start, TV-am had gone wrong by assuming that we all wanted to watch intellectuals or glamorous people at breakfast. The reality was that we wanted the equivalent of a chat over the garden fence with a neighbour,' says television critic Gordon Wood. And Lorraine was exactly the kind of unthreatening person you could imagine living next door. There was a sense that she might know a bit more than you did about current affairs but that wasn't very intimidating because she also seemed to know just as much about soap and pop stars. 'She was the kind of person you could gossip and share your problems with. Her accent might have put a few people off at first but when we got used to that we decided we liked her. And likeability is an incredibly valuable currency in television.'

Other critics said there were other reasons why Lorraine's everywoman appeal found its ideal home on breakfast television. 'Most people watch Lorraine Kelly while they are doing something else,' pointed out the *Daily Mail*'s Jeremy Hodges. 'You're feeding the kids and getting them ready for school, you're looking for your house keys, packing your bags for work. It's the most stressful time of the day and throughout it all Lorraine offers a voice of normality that you would miss if it wasn't there.'

* * * * *

As 1991 got underway, and Lorraine quietly celebrated the end of her first year as a mainstream national television presenter, she faced good and bad news at home and at work. Both events would help shape the rest of her life. The good news came when she won her first major broadcasting award. At a ceremony at the Grosvenor House Hotel on London's Park Lane the Television and Radio Industries Club named her New Talent of the Year, for her roles on *Good Morning Britain*, on TV-am's early-morning shows the previous year, and for her in-the-field reporting role in Scotland. The Tric awards are only just acquiring a high profile among the general public but for more than thirty years they have been hugely prestigious to industry insiders. The list of past winners includes almost every big name presenter and entertainer you can name. So Lorraine was thrilled to be recognised in such fantastic company at what was still only the start of her studio-based career. It gave her the confidence to feel that she did indeed deserve her place on the TV-am sofa. The cub reporter from East Kilbride had come a long way, and she was still loving every minute of the ride.

Lorraine and Steve celebrated with a long weekend away – they headed to one of their favourite spots in the whole world: Barra in the Outer Hebrides. Here they walked along the white beaches, chatted to the locals, had a glass of whisky and watched the sun go down over the ocean. It was the perfect place to reflect on how fast their lives were changing and to try and chill out away from the pressures of work. Lorraine says a few days away in Scotland always give her a new sense of perspective about the world and her role in it. She says that she doesn't spend her breaks planning ahead, plotting her next move or setting up some new long-term challenge. Instead, she tries to relax and be grateful for where she is right now.

Heading back south after this latest break she was about to get some bad news, however. Her much-loved grandmother, Margaret McMahon, had been given a late diagnosis of breast cancer. The news had come too late for much to be done. And on Margaret's death, Lorraine found a cause she would support personally and professionally for the rest of her life. Over the coming decades she would help raise hundreds of thousands of pounds for breast cancer charities. Equally importantly, she has tried to raise the profile of the disease and to make sure women know just how important early diagnosis can be. Her grandmother's death changed her in one other way too. Margaret McMahon had always been an extraordinary role model to her granddaughter. She had had a zest for life, and a desire to focus on all that was positive in the world and to make the most of every opportunity that came her way. 'Seize the day,' had been Margaret's motto. It would now be Lorraine's. She would no longer take anything for granted, she would enjoy every moment as if it was her last.

5

WEDDING BELLS

'It was a brilliant party and I was the last to leave it.'

It was just after 8am on Tuesday, 28 April 1992 and Ulrika Jonsson had finished giving her weather report. Everything had gone well and as usual she looked across the TV-am studio to hand back over to Lorraine and Mike Morris. But on this particular morning it turned out that Mike hadn't quite finished with her.

'Ulrika, before you go, can we perhaps have a forecast for 5 September?' he asked, hardly able to take a strangely cheeky smile off his face and flashing a quick grin at his co-presenter as he spoke.

There was an embarrassed pause from Ulrika at the other end of the studio. 'Shall we tell them?' she asked, finally, looking not at Mike but at Lorraine. After yet another rare pause, Lorraine finally spoke. 'You naughty man!' she admonished Mike, giving him a couple of pretend slaps with her hand and starting to giggle even louder than normal. The cameramen, suddenly realising what was going on, began to focus in on Lorraine's left hand. For she was wearing an engagement ring; 5 September had just been set for her late-summer wedding. The weather, Ulrika confidently predicted, would be good.

'I'll be known as Mrs Smith,' was all Lorraine would say that morning about the identity of her husband-to-be, though everyone in the studio knew full well that it had been Steve who had popped the question. After nearly seven years together, and after far too long trying to split their worlds between Scotland and London, the pair had decided to begin a new chapter of their joint lives. Steve was being offered increasing amounts of work in London so a move south looked inevitable. Both were thrilled about the prospect of living together seven days a week again, just as they had when they first met. Both wanted to be married.

In the run-up to the big day they had to put up with some typically unromantic comment from several newspapers, however. When news of their engagement broke, several reporters ignored the couple's long heritage together. Instead they simply labelled Lorraine as yet another cliché case of a television presenter falling in love with her cameraman – Ulrika Jonsson, Carol Barnes and Kathryn Holloway all being used as other examples of the genre. 'These are relationships born of insecurity and dependency,' one paper proclaimed. 'Cameramen can make women look ghastly with the wrong light or angles. Female presenters become dependent on their favourite cameramen and a relationship develops of trust and need. There is also a general arousal or frisson in a TV studio, especially if it is live. The emotions of excitement overlap with those of sexual passion. One emotion enhances the other.'

Having read the article, Lorraine, Steve and the friends

and colleagues who went out for a celebratory meal together that spring hooted with laughter at the idea of TV-am's studios being a hotbed of sexual passion. At 6am, with a long, live show stretching ahead, sex was normally the last thing on anyone's mind, they joked. Equally amusing to them all was the idea of Lorraine being 'insecure and dependent' on Steve. Everyone who got to know them said both were clearly equal partners in the relationship. Steve, who is a keen five-a-side football player as well as a fan, can hold his own in any argument and has a joke for most occasions. The pair were a perfect fit, though as the wedding approached Steve made it clear that he didn't just want to stay behind the cameras, he wanted to stay behind the scenes as well. Thrilled with his wife-to-be's success and immensely proud of her on-screen work he had no wish to join her on photo-shoots, magazine interviews or celebrity profiles. 'No comment,' are two of the very few words he has ever said to the press over the years.

Just before their wedding day Lorraine wanted to surprise her mum by inviting her to one big public event. She had long since ditched her Fearless Fly glasses and spent £70 on a more discrete, tortoiseshell-framed pair that she wore on the days when her eyes were too dry for contact lenses. Few other presenters wore glasses on screen, and Lorraine was named Spectacle Wearer of the Year. As awards go it might not have had the prestige of the New Talent of the Year award from the Television and Radio Industries Club. However, Lorraine's fellow winner was Cliff Richard and because she knew her mum had always dreamed of meeting him she put her wedding plans on hold so that Anne could travel down to London for the photo-shoot she did with the singer. 'Mum was far more impressed at meeting Cliff than she was by almost anything else I ever won,' Lorraine says with a smile.

By the first weekend of September 1992, everyone's attention was firmly back on the wedding venue. As Madonna and Guy Ritchie were to do later, they were getting married in a Scottish castle. But this was where all the similarities ended. Unlike the distant Skibo Castle that the pop star was to pick for her big day, Lorraine and Steve had gone for the far more accessible Main Castle in Dundee's Caird Park. It was in Steve's home city and having spent so many weekends there during the past seven years it felt like Lorraine's second home too. They had huge numbers of friends and family in the city and wanted to make it as easy as possible for everyone to share their special day.

From the very start, Lorraine had decided there would be none of the distractions that can take the romance out of many big name weddings. There would be no heavy security at Mains Castle, no exclusive deals to publish photographs in celebrity magazines, no bans on guests taking their own pictures or asking for autographs. Instead, she wanted a good old-fashioned wedding to remember. She says she was almost tearful when she saw how members of the public turned up early in the day armed with lucky horseshoes and flowers to wish her all the best. So she was happy to chat to as many of the well-wishers as possible, both before and after the ceremony.

Not surprisingly, her oldest friend Joyce was her chief bridesmaid, while several of her newer TV-am pals, including Mike Morris, were among the guests. Steve, Lorraine's dad and many of the other men wore kilts while Lorraine wore an £800 dress – not exactly pushing the boat out when you compare it with the dresses worn at most 'celebrity weddings' but still the most expensive item of clothing she had ever bought. 'I had fallen in love with it. It had tight sleeves pointed in a medieval style, very plain and simple. I wanted to wear something elegant and it was a very special wedding,' she says.

Several of the people in Caird Park who applauded as they got their first glance of Lorraine in the dress, said they were surprised at how tiny she looked. But while 5ft 4in Lorraine had wanted to wear high heels on her big day she was so unsteady on them that she had the dress altered so that she could go back to her usual flats.

When the time came for Steve to give Lorraine her ring, the couple were also acting true to form. Their choice was typically modest – it had cost just £150 and the pair had bought it at an airport in the south of France on the way back from a work trip earlier in the year. Lorraine's view had been that money was the least important factor in choosing something like a ring. Having found something she loved, and perhaps more importantly, having spotted it on a day when she and Steve had been feeling utterly happy and relaxed, meant more to her than any fancy packaging or price tag. She told friends that the ring would always bring layers of happy memories to her. So, as far as she was concerned, it was priceless.

After the ceremony the fun really started. Lorraine threw herself into the crowds of guests trying to make sure she spoke to as many people as possible. She waved at, talked to and was photographed with literally dozens of people, making no distinction between family, friends and fans. The wedding breakfast was long and hilarious, and the evening's entertainment unique. As the highpoint of the night the couple had hired The Clan, a group who dress up as Highlanders and put on noisy mass battles. Drink and dancing followed, giving Lorraine even more reasons to be pleased she hadn't tried to wear high heels. 'It was a brilliant party and I was the last to leave it,' she remembers with a huge smile.

What she also laughs about is the fact that her honeymoon was as disaster-prone as almost all the couple's overseas trips. Their original idea had been to chill out far from any madding crowds in the Florida Keys. But September was the hurricane season and a big one had hit just before their flight was due to leave Scotland, throwing all their plans into disarray. Instead of a couple of weeks on the very grown-up Hemingway trail Lorraine and Steve were re-routed to Orlando, where they joined the throngs of families and children at Disneyland and all the other theme parks. Even this brought extra drama – in one hotel they woke up having been attacked by swarms of flea-like bugs and needed to find a doctor for cortisone injections to dull the pain and make them look a little better in their honeymoon photographs.

* * * * *

Lorraine had managed to take her mind off work entirely for the duration of her honeymoon. But as she and Steve flew back to Britain she knew she was flying into a storm of uncertainty. The previous year the Government had put the breakfast television franchises up for auction to the highest bidder. It had triggered a hugely uncertain time for everyone, not least the TV-am bosses who had no idea how much cash to put up to retain their right to broadcast. In the autumn of 1991, it became clear that they hadn't offered enough. TV-am had its bid rejected and was told that on 1 January 1993 a new company would take over production of ITV's breakfast shows. Its name was GMTV, and when Lorraine headed back to work after her honeymoon, staff were finally waking up to the fact that the decision wasn't going to be reversed. At this stage, no one really knew what GMTV's plans were, what kind of shows it would produce or, most importantly, who it would employ to make them.

In its final autumn, the mood beneath the plastic egg cups at TV-am's Camden studios varied from panic to relief to depression. Rumours abounded about the new company's intentions and each would trigger a fresh wave of hopes and fears. One day everyone would be told that the status quo would be maintained and that all the TV-am staff would switch seamlessly on to new GMTV contracts. The next day someone would say they had heard that an entirely new team of producers and presenters were being recruited in America to shake up the UK industry from 1 January. The day after that a completely different story would do the rounds.

It was little wonder, then, that the atmosphere behind the scenes at TV-am was becoming so highly charged. Almost every day people announced they were leaving for safer jobs elsewhere. Others were finding it hard to focus on the job in hand and risked letting standards slip. Lorraine, though, was determined to offer show business as usual. She wanted to make sure that viewers were shielded from the office politics going on in the wings. In the process she won some powerful fans among television executives who recognised a professional, and a fighter, when they saw one.

But after a while, even Lorraine started to feel the pressure of keeping up appearances in public. Psychiatrists say that getting married, moving house and losing your job are three of the most stressful life changes people go through. As the uncertainty over TV-am's future raged in the autumn of 1992, Lorraine felt as if she was going for the triple. With their wedding out of the way, she and Steve had decided it was time to buy a new house together in the south and Lorraine was trying to squeeze in as many viewings as possible when her schedule allowed. She was also heading back to their existing home in Dundee every weekend to spend time with her new husband. And she was trying to hedge her bets and scout out new employment opportunities in advance of the new breakfast regime starting in 1993. Little wonder that the girl who described herself as a 'pit pony' at work suddenly let her defences down.

'I was travelling 1,000 miles every weekend to see Steve in Dundee. I was working neurotic hours when TV-am was just coming to an end and we didn't know if we were going to be in or out of a job the following year. I think my body started to say: "Hold on, enough is enough," and I came down with shingles, which I think I got from a lad who had chicken pox at a barbeque I had just been to with Steve. The doctor reckoned I had come down with it because I was rundown and stressed, and he practically frog-marched me to the studio door and ordered me to take two weeks off.'

As usual, Lorraine tried to tell him she didn't need to. She was worried about letting her colleagues down and concerned that with so much uncertainty going on this was the very worst time to be out of the studio. But by then the shingles had caught hold and began to hurt. She started to scratch to try and dull the pain and only made it worse. Steve and her parents said she had to follow the doctor's orders so the couple took a last-minute flight to Cyprus, where they lay in the sun and gave Lorraine's body a chance to recover. As she tried to relax overseas, she realised the illness was more than just a physical shock. She prided herself on never having been a patient in hospital since the day she had been born and joked that she was such a rare visitor to her doctor that he could be excused for thinking she had moved house. 'I normally soak up stress like a sponge but everyone has their limits,' she says of her sudden vulnerability.

By the time a fully recovered Lorraine got back to work, her agent had some good – and secret – news to pass on. She had been offered a job with the new company, so would still be on screen in 1993. The bad news was that she would be working with an almost entirely new group of people. As far as her agent was aware, no one else from TV-am was going to be taken on by GMTV. All of Lorraine's colleagues were about to have their worst fears confirmed and be out of work in the New Year.

As you might expect, this meant the atmosphere at TV-am became even more strained. Christmas was around the corner but very few people felt like celebrating. And Lorraine was desperately unhappy. 'There was a real sense of camaraderie at TV-am; we were like a family. It takes time to build up that kind of atmosphere and it was a huge shame, such a waste, to lose it,' she said as the year-end approached. What was also a huge waste, she said privately, was the fact that the plug was being pulled on TV-am just when it was doing so well. She and Mike were enjoying record ratings on *Good Morning Britain*. Critics and audiences were in rare agreement that the show was going well. Even Margaret Thatcher wrote a letter to the station's boss saying how upset she was that it was going off the air.

But 31 December 1992 was its final day. And Lorraine didn't have any doubts about what to wear. She picked her favourite deep red tartan jacket and skirt – one of the signature outfits that she wore whenever she wanted a confidence boost. In her shared dressing room just after 6am she looked at herself in the mirror. It was the right choice, she felt, because she wanted the day to look like a party rather than a wake. It was also pretty good because, after all, it was Hogmanay. With her hair tied back in a sparkling clip she chose some long, equally sparkling earrings and got ready for the show. 'I hope this mascara is waterproof because I can't guarantee I won't cry,' she told her long-standing make-up team as they worked on their favourite client for the very last time.

Then the cameras rolled. 'It is of course a very special day for us at TV-am, the very last programme after nine years and eleven months of bringing you Britain's brightest and best breakfast TV service,' Lorraine said, desperately trying to sound cheerful as the opening credits to the show faded away.

What the audience didn't know was that for so early in the morning the TV-am studio was unusually full. More than 400 crew members, presenters, former presenters and favourite celebrity guests were crowding the building, many of them standing right behind the cameras as Lorraine and Mike tried to carry on with the show. Co-presenter Kathryn Holloway lifted the mood and kept everyone's spirits up by announcing she was expecting a baby, and with 300 bottles of champagne waiting to be drunk and a huge bacon and eggs brunch from outside caterers waiting to be served the post-show party was expected to be good.

But before then, everyone had to try and get through the

show without crying. Lorraine was the first to crack. 'It's nearly time to say goodbye and it's high time we thanked you, the viewers, for your loyalty,' she began, before the tears started to well up in her eyes. She put her hand in front of her face and let Mike carry on with her vote of thanks. Minutes later, arm in arm with the man she had shared the sofa with for nearly three years, she was back in control. 'You're the biggest rogue of all,' she told Mike, giving him a kiss live on air as the final sign-off began. The whole gang of presenters waved goodbye as the TV-am theme tune played – to be replaced when transmission ended with Tina Turner's 'Simply the Best'.

The party lasted the rest of the morning and most of the afternoon before the staff finally started to drift away. Lorraine, for once not the last to leave, was in tears again as she walked out to the taxi waiting for her in the studio driveway. Under her arm she was holding a souvenir – the on-set clock she had looked at almost every day for the past four years. It has been in her house ever since.

6

THE F-FACTOR

*'The Cure's Robert Smith taught me
to drink vodka and cranberry juice because it
doesn't give you hangovers.'*

There was a lot of schoolboy sniggering about the launch of GMTV the following morning, 1 January 1993. Its executives had triggered a lot of double entendres when they explained why they had chosen their key presenters and what sort of image they were expected to live up to. The buzzword for the women was F-factor – with the letter F officially standing for 'fanciability' but unofficially being used as shorthand for something a little more basic – hence the sniggers.

The flagship show was called *Top Of The Morning*, and along with the rest of GMTV's programmes it was originally broadcast from Studio 5 at the former LWT Tower on the south bank of the River Thames in London. As far as Lorraine was concerned, leaving the old Camden studios was a wrench. She had loved the off-the-wall, individualistic feel of the former garage and she enjoyed heading off into the funky, grungy surroundings of Camden for lunch and a wander round the shops afterwards. But she had to admit that the south bank studios felt a whole lot more professional. The main sound stages were in the basement and lower floors of the building from where most of the biggest names in British entertainment had recorded shows over the years. Huge photographs of everyone from Morecambe and Wise to Bruce Forsyth adorned the walls on the walk from the lifts to the various studios, dressing rooms and offices. And it was a huge thrill later in the year when she had her own near life-size image put up alongside them.

In the early days of GMTV, Lorraine wasn't the main host of the breakfast show, however, and it was easy to overlook her in the post-launch publicity. On the very first show of the new regime viewers saw Eamonn Holmes and Anne Davies sitting behind a formal round table and in front of a supposedly roaring log fire. 'Good morning. A new day, a new year, a new television station. Welcome to GMTV, Britain's brightest start,' was how Eamonn introduced things. He and Anne promised to be first with the news, with the entertainment stories and with the fun that breakfast viewers expected. At 6am on Monday, 4 January the new weekday presenters, Fiona Armstrong and Michael Wilson, were there saying: 'There's something for everyone – news, interviews, entertainment and fun for the children as well.' But whether it was Fiona and Michael from Monday to Thursday or Eamonn and Anne on a Friday, there was a lot of tension behind the scenes and in the GMTV boardroom. The search for the F-factor was putting too much pressure on people and sexual chemistry was in short supply. Audiences were slumping to dangerous lows, money was tight and after just a few months in the hot seat Fiona Armstrong was ready to quit.

So what – or more importantly, who – could save GMTV?

The bosses commissioned a huge piece of detailed, sensitive and supposedly top-secret research into all its current and prospective presenters. Their key aim was to find the three or four most admired and respected names from which they could make their final selection as Fiona's replacement. But when the results came in everyone received a shock. There weren't three or four equally popular presenters out there. There was just one dominant player and a long list of also-rans – which worryingly enough included some of the best-known and best-paid presenters in the business.

The most admired presenter and the one that beat all the others by a mile was Lorraine Kelly.

* * * * *

Having been partially buried on the GMTV's early shows since the start of 1993, Lorraine was given her big promotion, teaming up first with Michael Wilson and then with Eamonn Holmes on *Top Of The Morning*. Lorraine Kelly was once more the saviour, and the biggest star, of breakfast television. But she treated it all with her typical humour. 'Funnily enough, nobody ever suggested I had the F-factor,' she joked afterwards as people asked about the changes at the channel. But this, of course, was the point.

'When GMTV started it was supposed to be all about very sexy, very glamorous presenters – and the one who outlasted them all was Lorraine, the one with the heavy fringe, the glasses and the giggle and accent that could drive some people mad,' said media studies lecturer Michael Hatton. 'The previous presenters weren't all swans and Lorraine is no ugly duckling. But it is ironic all the same that the channel where looks were deemed to be so important would end up being saved by the one presenter who seemed not to give two hoots about her appearance.' The other thing that changed with Lorraine's promotion was the GMTV set. Out went the formal table and harsh, modernistic fireplace. In their place came the sofas and the relaxed, comfortable feel. The presenter was back in her TV-am element. She was having fun, and it showed.

'They were good shows to make and I think it was clear that we gave audiences the kind of stories and treatments that they wanted,' she says of the early GMTV days. 'Our aim every morning was to respond to the issues and subjects that viewers were already thinking about, or to point them in the direction of the kind of things they could talk over with anyone they spoke to later in the day. We both followed and set the agenda and it worked because we were all so relaxed and genuinely interested in it ourselves.' It was water-cooler television, nearly a decade before the term had even been invented.

Ratings spiked up from the post-launch lows and GMTV was on its way to becoming a new national institution, with a sense of fun and zest that the BBC's revamped *Breakfast* show would take a long time to match. While her stock was high, Lorraine started taking a few steps up the celebrity ladder. She joined the likes of Richard Madeley, Tom Baker, Susan George and Ruth Madoc in an episode of the murder-mystery gameshow *Cluedo*. She sat and giggled away alongside Jo Brand when the pair were both invited on to the *Mrs Merton Show*. Back at breakfast, Lorraine gradually worked her way through a list of celebrity interviews that was already starting to rival that of Michael Parkinson. Throw in an obligatory tussle with Rod Hull and Emu (Lorraine ended up falling off the end of her own breakfast sofa in what would be one of the most repeated clips of the year) and her position in the entertainment A-list was fast being assured.

Her reputation for hard work was also getting noticed. As soon as *Top Of The Morning* finished broadcasting she took out her contact lenses, got on with her paperwork and planning for the next show, and then started to tackle her other challenges. Chief among them was her long-running search for a permanent base south of the border. She had hugely enjoyed living in Notting Hill when she had first come down to London for TV-am and had stayed in west London ever since. She told friends she still felt like a city girl and was terrified of stagnating or going soft out in the suburbs. But in the back of her mind she was hoping that she and Steve might soon start a family and so she knew it made sense to consider somewhere they could afford a detached house with its own garden. A weekend dinner party with Ulrika Jonsson helped her decide exactly where that house might be.

'Ulrika was always saying I should look around close to where she lived, because it was such a nice area and it was so easy to get into work,' says Lorraine. But until that dinner party the area's reputation as 'luvvie-land central' had put her off. Ulrika lived near Maidenhead in Berkshire close to the likes of Frank Bough, Michael Parkinson and Rolf Harris. Locals from yesteryear included Faye Dunaway, Dusty Springfield, Roger Moore, and even someone else whose career had been given a big boost by TV-am – the late Diana Dors.

When the likes of colleague Kathy Taylor and friend Carol Vorderman joined Ulrika in pushing the benefits of Berkshire, Lorraine and Steve finally gave in and got serious about doing the rounds with local estate agents. While both had always lived in cities they soon realised that life could be lived well on a smaller scale. Lorraine soon fell in love with the nearby towns of Marlow and Windsor, and could easily imagine herself ambling around the shops there on a weekend or exploring the local countryside for the perfect village pub.

First, all she needed was the perfect house to call her home. She and Steve looked at dozens and left each one feeling distinctly uninspired. Then they struck gold. One of their agents suggested a seventeenth-century property, formed years earlier from two workmen's cottages that had been knocked into one. It had low ceilings, original features and a wonderful atmosphere. Lorraine instantly knew that she wanted to live in it. 'As soon as I walked into the house I knew it was right for us. I just felt it had a very happy atmosphere. I liked the sense of history and the feeling that so many people had lived here before,' she told friends.

It cost £200,000 back in 1993, more than three times the national average of the day. But as a double-income, no-kiddies family Lorraine and Steve had no problem paying the bills. As they unpacked and started to feel at home Lorraine also acquired a new hobby. She started to look through the paperwork that the solicitor had sent as part of the purchase, flicking through the copy of the deeds and imagining the lives of all the people who had lived in their home before them. If I ever have the time to research and write it up properly it could make a wonderful book, one day, she thought.

* * * * *

Finding time was still a huge challenge, however, and getting up before 5am didn't always feel as if it made the days much longer. One problem was that Lorraine was still being sent on plenty of roving assignments – all good fun, but all eating into what little spare time she had.

Just after moving house, she was given the chance to relive her days as a teenage Goth by interviewing one of her music heroes, The Cure's Robert Smith. The only problem was that the interview wasn't going to be done in half an hour in the GMTV studios. 'They were on their way to America but because Robert didn't like flying they were sailing across instead,' Lorraine remembers. So she and a film crew were put on the QEII to join them. 'It was a huge thrill for me to meet him and he taught me to drink vodka and cranberry juice because it doesn't give you hangovers,' Lorraine says.

She also remembers that she and Robert shared a uniquely bizarre showbusiness moment on the voyage. 'We were having a drink, standing at the bar, with Robert in all his huge hair and lipstick. In front of us were all these old disco ladies with glittery tops dancing away – and then The Cure's "Lovecats" came on and they were all getting on down.'

'This, Lorraine, is surreal,' Robert said to her, as they slipped quietly away.

Back from this trip, she was soon off on another one. Every year Lorraine tries to squeeze in at least one girlie weekend away with Joyce and her other old pals – saying the best-ever weekend came when they went to Paris, ate and drank constantly and ended up dancing on the bar at a club called Whisky-a-GoGo.

* * * * *

Back in the studio, Lorraine and Eamonn were relaxing into what would be an enduring, if sometimes unlikely, screen partnership. Both were guilty of talking over the other, and neither liked being interrupted. But they muddled through, able to joke and laugh like the old married couple many viewers apparently assumed they were. That said, the relaxed way the pair chatted on screen did sometimes cause problems for Lorraine – not least when she inadvertently ended up 'insulting' one of the biggest film stars of the day. The bizarre controversy arose in the spring of 1994 when the pair were set to do a joint interview with Julia Roberts. She was in the country to promote her latest film *The Pelican Brief*, and Eamonn and Lorraine were talking about it just before the actress arrived on the set.

'She is just such a beautiful woman. Just beautiful,' Lorraine cooed, echoing the thoughts of just about every viewer in the country. But, for reasons which were never quite made clear, this comment drove Julia Roberts' American staff wild. 'I was dismayed to hear your host ramble on about Ms Roberts' beauty. In this country, the behaviour that was evidenced on your programme is regarded as unprofessional,' GMTV was told immediately after the broadcast in an extraordinary fax sent from Hollywood.

'But Julia Roberts is beautiful, so why not say so?' GMTV's spokesman told the papers in Lorraine's defence as the bizarre war of words rumbled on.

Being supported by the company after spats like this meant a huge amount to Lorraine, and by the mid 1990s, she was starting to feel that GMTV had begun to develop the same sort of family atmosphere that she had so enjoyed at TV-am. People who work on breakfast television shows say friendships form relatively easily because everyone in the studio tends to have two key things in common – an obsession with sleep and an ongoing sense of exhaustion.

'Until you start getting up at 4am or earlier every day you don't realise just how much these topics will dominate your thoughts and your conversations,' says former GMTV producer Katie Hannah. 'We all talked endlessly about our various strategies to get more and better sleep, and it is a common bond that ties you to people that you might not get on well with in any other circumstances. Breakfast television is an entirely different world to any other part of the entertainment industry. It's a small, closed world and some of the friendships you make in it have proven to last long after you go back into a job with more ordinary hours.'

* * * * *

Lorraine agrees that the early-morning camaraderie can make the awful hours seem a lot more bearable. In fact she reckoned the happy atmosphere at GMTV ended up helping her to become pregnant – with an unwitting Eamonn getting most of the credit.

'We were all talking away as usual and one day Eamonn said we should all do something to get fit,' she says. 'So we started going to Mr Motivator, following some of his routines and having a bit of fun. Eamonn soon fell by the wayside but I carried on and got really fit for the first time in ages. I think that is probably why I conceived that September – I was just feeling so healthy all the time.'

With her pregnancy publicly acknowledged by the end of 1993, Lorraine set about breaking some taboos. She felt that pregnancy was not an illness, so why hide it? 'I was looking like a giant Easter egg on screen but I didn't mind one bit. I worked right up until the birth, getting bigger and bigger. It was quite unusual to see a pregnant presenter on television at that time but I wanted to carry on working. Soon afterwards, of course, Ulrika presented *Gladiators* looking gorgeous, glamorous and obviously pregnant, so we have moved on in our attitudes.'

Bad luck meant that Steve was working in Belfast for much of Lorraine's pregnancy. But when he was back in Berkshire he was ready to deal with his wife's unusual food cravings – including once going out to buy eight tins of mandarin oranges in syrup (and then going back to the shop to change them when Lorraine realised she wanted oranges in their own juice instead). It was the first of many such visits to the supermarket – because for a while, Lorraine said, she started eating as if she was expecting quads. Fortunately, she says she avoided some of the most common problems with pregnancy – heavy morning sickness would have been a bit of a problem when presenting a breakfast television show.

And with her mum and dad making plenty of visits to look after her, and with Joyce now living locally after getting a job running a club in the home counties, Lorraine had plenty of support as her due date approached. At home she would lie down resting the music box Steve had bought her on her bump, hoping that it relaxed and inspired their baby. At work she mostly felt energised rather than exhausted – she loved the fact that there were plenty of existing mums behind the scenes at GMTV ready to give her advice, as well as plenty of hopeful mums wanting to hear how she was coping.

But when the big moment came Lorraine was in for a shock. The woman who says she has spent her whole life in a hurry discovered that childbirth was one thing even she couldn't rush. Her labour lasted eighteen hours before baby

Rosie finally arrived on Wednesday, 8 June weighing 6lb 10.5oz. Steve was right there at her side and Lorraine says he hardly closed his eyes. 'He wasn't squeamish at all, probably because he had filmed lots of operations, though of course it is different when it is your own wife in the delivery room. Like most men he felt a bit helpless but I am so glad he was there. When Rosie finally arrived he shed a manly tear and I was howling.'

Steve also scored top marks for saying exactly the right thing at a crucial moment just after the birth. 'My hair hadn't been cut in ages – it was in a ponytail – and I was all sweaty and hugely fat. Yet just after we had hugged Rosie he turned to me and said: "You have never looked more beautiful," which was a total lie but absolutely wonderful,' she remembers with a smile.

For her part, Lorraine admits to going through a few crises of confidence during her long labour. She was almost twice as old as her mother had been when she herself had been born. But still she wasn't sure if she was ready for the challenges which lay ahead.

'Even when I was giving birth I was thinking: I'm not grown up enough for this! I was also very aware that I had never felt maternal before Rosie was born. I had just thought of babies as rather strange creatures and didn't really know one end from the other. Even when I was pregnant I couldn't really understand what having a baby meant.'

Fortunately, at the end of her labour all these doubts disappeared. 'I was astounded at how I felt. I looked at Rosie as soon as she was born and thought: Bloody hell, you look exactly the way I thought you would – it's you! I was overwhelmed by her from the moment she was born.'

7

BEING A MUM

'I was a blob. I was a mum. I ate chocolate Hob Nobs
all day and I absolutely loved it!'

L orraine's family and friends saw immediate changes in the
new mum after Rosie was brought home. 'Lorraine is as
happy now as I have ever seen her,' old friend Joyce said, after
spending time with mum and daughter and watching them
settle down to their new lives together. 'She is calm about
motherhood and just tremendously happy.'

But while Lorraine entirely agreed with the description of
her as happy, she wasn't so sure about the word calm. As
usual she had a million thoughts running through her mind.
She was also thinking ahead. 'When Rosie was born my mum
came racing down from Scotland and I said: "Mum, tell me
what you did with me because I'll do the same. I want Rosie
to be as happy as I was growing up."'

In the meantime, her position as one of the highest-profile
new mums in the country was putting her under extra
pressure. In typical fashion she had refused to consider the
increasingly common practice of doing a deal with a celebrity

magazine and offering pictures of her baby to the highest bidder. But she couldn't ignore the fact that so many well-wishers had followed all the ups and downs of her pregnancy and were thrilled over the news of Rosie's birth. A one-off appearance on the GMTV sofa was probably called for.

'Literally hundreds of people had knitted things and sent cards which was wonderfully kind so I kind of felt I owed it to them to bring Rosie into the studio,' Lorraine says. Just over a week after the birth she did just that. Rosie slept through most of her first public outing and almost everyone in the south bank studios commented on her shock of black hair.

With this event over, Lorraine and Steve decided to take a tough line with the media over their daughter. In the years ahead, Lorraine would talk endlessly about Rosie on her television and radio shows. But she refused to let her be photographed and made huge efforts to ensure her daughter was never taken to places where the paparazzi might be present. Children deserve their privacy, she said, even if one or both of their parents have chosen a more public life. When these children become adults they too might choose to embrace the celebrity culture, but until then they should be allowed to live in private. That's why for years she turned down almost all invitations to family-friendly film premières and other public events. A huge critic of people who use their families to promote their own careers, she says she couldn't stand the hypocrisy of demanding privacy on one day if she and her family had paraded in front of the cameras at some public event on another.

Back in 1994, though, Lorraine had no time to parade in front of anyone. She was at home being a mum and she was loving it. Funnily enough, she says her career to date turned out to have offered some subtle training for her new role, not least because early morning wake-up calls and sleep deprivation weren't much of a problem for someone who had been on breakfast television since the mid 1980s. In all other respects, she says, she just couldn't believe how happy and how lucky she was.

'For the first two months I lived in a red tartan dressing gown and didn't wash my hair. I was a blob. I was a mum. I ate chocolate Hob Nobs all day and I absolutely loved it,' she says with a laugh. But the career girl who had been working full time since the age of eighteen admits that motherhood was a surprisingly tricky assignment.

'Basically I realised I had to learn to let things go because I'm terribly organised and neat, and I couldn't keep control in the way I always had done. But I would say to any woman that if you are lucky enough to have the choice – and I know so many women don't – then spend as much time as you possibly can with your baby, as those first few months in particular are a magic time and you can never get that back.'

* * * * *

Determined to follow her late grandmother's advice, to seize the day and to enjoy every moment of her new life, Lorraine was happy to let go of other rules that had previously governed her life – not least the ones surrounding food. She had cleaned up her act during her pregnancy, eating plenty of fruit, vegetables and chicken. But with Rosie around other things seemed more important, and quick and easy comfort food seemed her easiest option again. It soon began to show.

'I had weighed about 10st since the age of eighteen, which was a bit heavy when you are just 5ft 4in, but then I always knew I was never going to be a model girl,' she says. 'I was never going to be slim because I always had a round tummy and a bottom and because I always had boobies. I was always curvy, that's the way I'm supposed to be.'

During her pregnancy Lorraine saw her weight go up to around 12? stone, but as she lost a stone straight after the birth she felt the rest would probably just follow, so she admits she took her eye off the ball. 'Everyone said breast-feeding would make the rest drop off me, but I just kept putting more weight back on. I ballooned.'

True to form, Lorraine was happy to accept full responsibility for the changes. 'I used the whole birth thing as an excuse to pig out and I just went mad. In hospital I started drinking three or four cups of Ovaltine a day. I would have mountains of toast with butter and whole packets of Hob Nob biscuits. If Steve brought me a chocolate orange I would eat the whole thing. Once I was out of hospital I tucked into sausage rolls and curries.'

At that time, being larger didn't affect her self-esteem because she was so wrapped up in Rosie. There were too many other things on Lorraine's mind, including trying to balance having a new baby and thinking about getting back to work. 'I also believe that when you've just had a baby you should enjoy yourself and not be too preoccupied by your shape. But my problem was that I went right off the rails.'

Lorraine's other problem was more selfless. Right back from her days on the *East Kilbride News* she had covered stories about anorexic girls and women, and had become incredibly sensitive about the kind of messages she and the rest of the media put out about weight and size. 'If I go on and on about being too big as a new mum then won't I just be reinforcing the old message that it's wrong to be large and that your weight matters more than anything else in your life?' she says. She decided she should keep quiet. The last thing she wanted was to encourage other women into dangerous diets. Anyway she was determined to stay out of the public eye for the whole of her GMTV maternity leave, so very few people knew she was still eating for two, several months after Rosie had been born.

When she did ease herself back into the world of work, she was able to stay in the shadows – the BBC had been in touch and asked if she wanted to fill in for a few afternoon shows on Radio Two over the late summer and early autumn. Always up for a new challenge and with her mum happy to babysit for a few hours once in a while, Lorraine said yes. Radio wasn't something she had spent much time doing before, but as she always says, she was born to talk. So in many ways she was a natural for the medium.

Over at Studio 5 on London's south bank the GMTV staff wanted Lorraine back as well. Rosie's birth had fitted in well with the summer schedule, as the main breakfast shows had been off the air for the holiday break during most of her maternity leave. But come September the new schedule was being drawn up and the bosses wanted Lorraine to play a big new part in it. After so many years as a co-presenter on the main breakfast sofa, they wanted to give Lorraine her own show. It was nearly time for viewers to see – and as it turned out to comment upon – the new look, larger-than-life Lorraine Kelly.

8

BACK IN BUSINESS

'So many chip shops, so little time.'

'Hello and welcome to *Nine O'Clock Live.*'
As far as Lorraine was concerned, absolutely everything was perfect about her new show – not least the fact that in starting at 9am it gave her a wonderful and unexpected lie-in. 'Getting up at 6 in the morning instead of 3.30 is fantastic. Anything before 4am is just a killer, like having jet lag permanently. This change alone means I now feel more like twenty six rather than thirty six,' she said after three months of the new routine. And she was characteristically grateful for being given the opportunity to shine at this new, later hour. 'GMTV have been fantastic since Rosie was born and there are not many people who can say that about their employer. Creating the new *Nine O'Clock Live* slot especially for me was wonderful, and I intend to enjoy every minute of it,' she said.

Unfortunately, when she looked up at the television monitors in the studio and caught sight of herself, she found her confidence fading away. 'I looked like a fat Italian mama, still wearing maternity dresses, leggings and maternity shirts months after the birth.' An even more galling wake-up call was to come, however. Lorraine had agreed to make a *Bringing Up Baby* video for GMTV, to help promote the new 'mother and baby' slots that were central to the early *Nine O'Clock Live* show. The channel's favourite doctor Hilary Jones was on hand along with some other experts and Lorraine was determined to make it a family affair. Steve did the filming and after much agonising the couple decided that Rosie should be part of the action as well.

Looking back, Lorraine says everyone's first challenge was to avoid patronising the audience. But with this in mind she was convinced that there was plenty of useful information to impart. The issue was simply to get the job done as sensitively as possible. 'Lots of people have babies, and I don't want to preach. It's not me saying: "This is how you should bring up a baby," I mean, what do I know?' she said, when critics asked her about the venture. 'But there are so many things you forget when you are a new parent. You are in the hospital and the midwife shows you how to bathe your baby, and you watch and say, oh yes, and then the minute you get home you've forgotten all about it. We just want to put all the information people need in one place so they can dip in and out of it whenever necessary.'

Ultimately, her key message for other new parents was simple. 'Relax, enjoy, and never be afraid to look ridiculous,' she said. The words came back to haunt her, however, when she and the crew filmed the final part of the video. It was a ten-minute fitness session for new mums and, of all things, Lorraine was handed a green leotard to wear when she presented it. In the editing suite she got a shock. 'To be honest it was really only then that I realised just how gigantic I had become. I was now apple-shaped with all the weight on my stomach, bottom, the tops of my arms and in my face.'

The GMTV staff she sat with when the footage was first shown weren't quite sure how to deal with their colleague's shock. For years they had been used to her joking happily about her appetite and her figure. 'So many chip shops, so little time,' was what one remembers as her favourite catch phrase. Another loves the story that when they were out on the road years earlier and needed a viewing screen, she had suggested that as her backside was the biggest thing in the room they might as well use that.

Suddenly, though, the time for jokes seemed to have passed. So Lorraine headed home puzzling about what she should do. Her first thought, pretty much out of character, was that some new clothes might make her feel better. But the rare shopping trip she took that weekend only ended up making things worse. 'I bought some size 12 trousers without trying them on. Not only did they not fit, but when I went back to the shop neither would the size 14. I couldn't believe it, but I also couldn't face up to the fact that I was going to have to buy a size 16 for the rest of my life. I decided enough was enough.'

Reading the newspapers was an equally unpleasant experience back then. As a new show, *Nine O'Clock Live* was widely reviewed, as was the *Bringing Up Baby* video. The critics were harsh. 'They say that the camera adds 10lb. Which only makes you wonder how many cameras they train on Lorraine Kelly every morning,' one particularly ungallant male wrote in the autumn of 1994. 'On screen, the girl from East Kilbride boasts all the solid, matriarchal physicality of a steamie's caretaker or a life-long stair-washer,' wrote another. Far from feeling thrity six, Lorraine suddenly started to feel forty six – or sometimes even older!

As it turned out, one final shock would have to come before she faced up to the inevitable and got serious about her diet and exercise regime. It had nothing to do with the image she saw on screen or in the mirror, but everything to do with the smiling face of the growing baby she saw at home. 'I was out one afternoon pushing Rosie around in her pram and I realised I was gasping for breath after going up some hills,' she says – quickly pointing out that the average gradients in Berkshire were hardly challenging. If I can't do this, how will I manage when I take Rosie back to Scotland to spend time with her grandparents? she asked herself. And what would happen as her girl got older? 'It suddenly dawned on me that when Rosie started to crawl she would want a mum who could do things with her. I wanted to be able to enjoy her without feeling exhausted. I was only thirty six but suddenly I felt like an old woman.'

So this, finally, was it and Lorraine turned to her family for advice on what to do next. Her cousin had been pregnant six months before her and had lost three stone and got her old figure back by the time Rosie had been born. Lorraine rang her up to find out her secret. 'It turned out that she had been to WeightWatchers, and so one Monday night in October I enrolled at my local club,' says Lorraine. 'I didn't feel embarrassed because everyone there was in the same boat. People looked at me at first, probably wondering if I was Lorraine Kelly or not, the way people often do, but after that I was just a member like everyone else.'

When she was weighed on her first visit, Lorraine was put

down as just over 11st 8lb. But she jokingly swears that was harsher than it should have been as she was wearing big boots that day. After doing her other measurements and talking things through with her class leader, her target weight was set at 9st 10lb – a tough target for anyone, but one Lorraine immediately swore she would meet. 'They put me on a special programme for breastfeeding mums and I was able to feed Rosie until she was eight and a half months old, which was wonderful.'

As far as she was concerned, 'special programme' was the right description for what she was doing. She says 'diet' is the one word she thinks should be banished from the English language because of the immediate sense of denial it conjures up in people. 'To fight against it I just said to myself: "I'm not on a diet, I'm just eating better," which took the pressure off and made it feel so much easier,' she says.

Her old friend Joyce was also on hand to keep Lorraine on the straight and narrow and out of the Hob Nob aisle. 'We've never been competitive with each other over anything except losing weight,' Joyce says. 'She will ring me up and go: I've lost half a stone. And I'll go: I hate you! But ultimately we do it to support each other, and it works.'

The other thing that had always worked in almost every part of Lorraine's life was to be busy. And this, of course, was to help once she threw out the Ovaltine and the chocolate biscuits and spent more time in her Marlow greengrocer's. Her new food routine began in late November and meant she started her day with a cup of tea at home, boosted her energy with some cereal and a banana in the studio shortly after 7.30am, then had pasta with tuna and a yoghurt for lunch. She had apples and bananas on hand in the afternoon in case she got hungry and made herself swear not to dip into the biscuit tin. And it all worked. After a decent initial weight dip, then a sudden New Year reversal, she fell below her 9st 10lb target weight by the following summer.

'Your legs look wonderful, I'm proud of you!' It was GMTV's fitness expert Mr Motivator (aka Derrick Errol Evans) who yelled the compliment at Lorraine one morning in the corridors of the London Television Centre after a show. At home, Steve was equally pleased – though he said the most important thing to him was his wife's new-found sense of wellbeing rather than her weight or figure. 'He doesn't want me to be too thin and even if he thought I looked like an elephant after having Rosie, he was kind enough never to say so,' Lorraine said at the time, making her viewers even more convinced that she had married the man of all their dreams.

The Monday night WeightWatchers classes also became part of Lorraine's routine, and her fellow classmates became good friends. 'We give each other advice, from what to wear at special events to clever recipes. One lady told me that instead of chocolate mousse she took a Cadbury's Options and put it in natural yoghurt. I used that tip so many times I almost made myself sick!'

Apart from feeling more bouncy, eating sensibly also gave her a chance to go back to something she had avoided since that one time after Rosie had been born – shopping. Fortunately, in 1995 she had an entirely different experience, a mirror image of her previous foray on the high street. That time, she had bought trousers in size 12 but found she only fitted into a size 16. This time, she was euphoric when she picked a size 16 off the rail and discovered they made her look as if she was wearing a clown's clothes. She tried the 14

– and they were still too big. So, hardly believing it, she reached for the size 12. She says it was like the clothes shop version of the shampoo advert where people hear a lady moan in ecstasy as she washes her hair. She jokes that she had to stop herself from moaning just as loud as she did a mini twirl in front of the dressing-room mirror. No longer would she have to worry whether her clothes covered her bottom or whether her stomach stuck out. She felt she could wear what she liked and carry it off. She felt fantastic – though she knew that it wasn't quite game over as far as her figure was concerned.

Like most people, her weight would fluctuate wildly in the years ahead, and she says keeping her weight off would ultimately prove even harder than losing it. That's why her weekly WeightWatchers classes lasted for another eighteen months, and she committed herself to returning as often as she felt she needed to in the future. She wanted to keep her focus on good food and to stop reaching for the Hob Nobs and the mini-Mars Bars when the going got tough. While WeightWatchers, almost by definition, focused on the story your bathroom scales told you about your body, Lorraine also came up with her own, very unique weight loss aid. It wasn't a tape measure or a weighing machine but a pair of tight black, size 12 leather trousers. In the years ahead, they would be her main weight watcher. If she can fit into them for a night out then all is well. If not, she needs to take some action. 'It's that simple, and it's that hard,' she says realistically.

As an extra incentive, Lorraine and Steve had just discovered a great place for her to show off her size 12 trousers. It was Chequers Brasserie, a fantastic restaurant in Cookham Dean, just a few stones' throws away from their house. The couple soon bonded with the owners and staff, and Lorraine was determined to keep her figure in shape so she could go there every now and again and splurge on the pan-fried monkfish, French cheeses, deep-fried Brie, chicken liver salad and homemade cheesecake that she felt beat almost anything you could get in far more expensive London restaurants.

Other local favourites included the Lemon Grass restaurant in Maidenhead, which Lorraine reckons makes one of the best Indian meals she has eaten and The Inn On The Green back in Cookham Dean for special occasions.

* * * * *

While her 6am starts for *Nine O'Clock Live* still felt like a lie-in, Lorraine's schedule meant that she and Steve could never hang around any of their local pubs or restaurants very late in the evenings, however. They were also heading back up to Scotland a little more often now that Rosie was crawling and ready to treat her grandparents' house as her second home. It was on one of those early visits that Lorraine met up with some producers from Scottish Television. They had a programme idea they wanted to discuss with her but they didn't have a lot of money to spend and were worried that she would turn them down as being out of hand. Their idea was for something a little harder-edged than her usual breakfast-time fare, and they were concerned that she might not want to leap out of her comfort zone.

But they shouldn't have worried. The show was to be called *Live Issue* and the more Lorraine was told about it, the more she wanted to work on it. It was to be shown in the middle of the evening, so it would be her first prime-time slot. While it was designed to be a magazine-style show, just like much of breakfast television, the aim was to tackle a series of topical and moral issues. And as long as she could play a full role in the writing and production rather than just turning up to read a script, then she was happy to be on board.

The first series was broadcast in Scotland in the early summer of 1995 and began with an examination of how parents, emergency service workers and others dealt with the death of loved ones and strangers. 'Lorraine Kelly is a lively talker, but above all she is a good listener,' said media expert Jeremy Hodges, who reviewed the show for the *Sunday Times*. He had some reservations about the programme, not least over the low budget, which he said showed in the too-easy choice of guests. But he wasn't able to fault its presenter and thought there might be even better television from her to come. 'She is flexing intellectual muscles no one knew she had,' wrote a fellow commentator, while Hodges concluded that: 'We could yet see another side to Lorraine Kelly that will surprise us all.'

As the summer progressed, other reporters were starting to think the same. That year, the *Daily Mail* had sent writer Sarah Chalmers up to Glasgow to watch Lorraine at work and to try and define what made her so popular. Chalmers' conclusions were interesting. 'Lorraine has been so successful at projecting the big sister persona that we forget she is, in fact, a very clever woman who has made it to the top of a very tough profession,' she said.

Not that Lorraine wanted this brought to anyone's attention. Sarah says the Lorraine she spent time with that summer was always trying to explain her success away as simple, old-fashioned good luck. But, after watching the presenter both on and off camera and seeing how she interacted with colleagues and the general public alike, the reporter refused to buy it. She watched as Lorraine wrote and re-wrote scripts right up to the moment the *Live Issue* cameras rolled; how she ensured she knew as much as possible about the subject under discussion and the people she was speaking to, and how this detailed preparation made her so capable of holding a live broadcast together. 'To sum up Lorraine's whole career as luck is a mistake and obscures a canny mind plus an incredible amount of hard work,' Chalmers concluded as she headed back down south.

After the first series of *Live Issue* went off air (Lorraine would come back to film two more in the coming years), she signed up for a more lightweight, but no less challenging proposition. The BBC had picked her to work alongside Scottish actor Gordon Kennedy and to be the main host of its *Hogmanay Live* show for New Year's Eve, 1995. Television insiders say winning such a high-profile role was a surprising coup for Lorraine because back then the BBC very rarely wanted to give top slots to any of ITV's big stars. But the bosses felt an exception had to be made for Lorraine and for Hogmanay. Everyone wanted to pull out all the stops as the big night approached.

'I can't believe you're making me wear a secondhand dress. Is money really this tight at the BBC?' Lorraine was sharing a joke as she sat in the dressing room of a west London photographic studio. The hair and make-up staff were getting her ready to model for some publicity shots for the New Year's Eve show, and the dress she was being asked to wear was far from any old hand-me-down. 'Can you believe it? The last person to wear this dress was one of the Bond girls in *Golden Eye*,' Lorraine crowed over the newly released 007 film.

'Nothing was going to stop me from squeezing into it because I've always wanted to be a Bond babe!'

There was less to laugh about as New Year's Eve arrived, however. The show was being broadcast live to the whole of the UK from Edinburgh Castle and insiders said it was turning out to be a lot more nerve-wracking than a typical day at GMTV. For some reason, New Year's Eve frequently brings out the worst in even the most experienced of producers and presenters, and the show has a reputation for being a career-stopper.

'Broadcasting history is littered with Hogmanay horrors,' says television critic and historian Andy Moran, explaining it as being something to do with the false bonhomie, the huge expectations as the countdown begins, and the fact that the presenters really ought to be sober when large numbers in their audience are drunk. 'History shows gremlins seem to come out to play on New Year's Eve. Satellite links and outside broadcasts that work perfectly 364 days of the year seem to break up on the big one. The last few minutes of these shows can feel like an eternity as desperate presenters try to fill in for all the technical hitches that are going on behind the cameras. Signing up to present the show can seem like a great idea in the autumn when you are hoping for one last big pay day of the year, but it may not seem such a good job to have when the countdown begins.'

As the crew went through the last pre-show checks inside Edinburgh Castle, Lorraine was praying that she had the experience to get the job done, however tense things got – which was exactly what the BBC was relying on, too. 'The fact that the show is live certainly doesn't bother me, in fact it makes it better for me,' she said of the challenge. 'I love doing live broadcasts, that's how my career started and what I have been working on pretty much ever since I joined TV-am. I prefer the kick you get out of being live and I've coped with enough behind-the-scenes disasters in my career so far to be ready for anything this night can throw at me.'

At midnight, as fireworks screamed into the Edinburgh sky and the broadcast drew to a close, it seemed as if the gremlins and the disasters had stayed away. But while no one's career had ended that night, it still felt as if the show had fallen a little flat. With a poor choice of live bands the critics said that Lorraine and Gordon had struggled to put any sparkle into the evening – and that some of the guests had been embarrassingly dull. The Scottish newspapers in particular were quick to criticise. 'The television companies turned Hogmanay viewing into Hootmanay,' concluded the *Daily Record*, for example.

And Lorraine couldn't avoid the comments by heading back south on New Year's Day – she is so keen to stay in touch with what her friends and family in East Kilbride and Dundee are thinking that she has all the Scottish papers delivered to her home every day. When she went round to other mums' houses in Berkshire, Lorraine says, the *Daily Mail* was the most popular paper she saw lying around. But when the local mums came round to hers they saw the *Daily Record* and the *Sunday Post*. She also likes to keep up to date on things north of the border by watching *Reporting Scotland* on digital television.

* * * * *

For links with her homeland, Lorraine went further than keeping up with the news. She extended the Scottish dimension of her home to the outside, by planting batches of heather in her otherwise very English country garden. Tartan wallpaper, she said, was the only thing she felt her house was lacking – but she was unable to find a shop that sold it.

Wallpaper apart, Lorraine's house had changed a lot over the past three years. When she and Steve had moved in, the converted cottages had been the perfect size for the two of them – and so soon after the demise of TV-am, they had been loathe to spend too much money on the property in case Lorraine found herself out of work like so many of her former colleagues. Since Rosie's arrival and the success of GMTV and Lorraine's other programmes, however, the pair had decided to splash out – quite literally. One of their first big changes was to have a heated swimming pool installed in the garden. And this was only the beginning. While Rosie was starting to crawl the family had the builders round and added a conservatory, an office, a big new garage and a greenhouse. They also hired garden designers to revamp the outside of the property and created a private courtyard as a family suntrap.

The one room they didn't know what to do with was the old air raid shelter at the back of the garden. For Lorraine, structures like this were like living history. They inspired her because they reminded her of the way the world had changed and the way populations adapted and survived great threats. So while some said the shelter should be filled in and forgotten, she was determined to keep it standing. She and Steve whitewashed the walls and left it there as a monument to the past. When she had time, she said, she would once more look through the property's lease to see who had lived there during the war years and get more of a picture of life when the shelter had been built.

Inside the house, Lorraine admits that not every change went exactly to plan. The new conservatory, for example, was supposed to be a peaceful oasis for the couple and their grown-up friends. 'I thought it would be nice to sit there on Sunday mornings and read the newspapers, and maybe to have the occasional gin and tonic in the afternoons,' says Lorraine.

As it turned out, the room was commandeered by Rosie and her tiny friends. It became a playroom, and the floor – which was reclaimed from a nearby gymnasium that was being demolished – is now covered in toys, games and worse. 'Rosie and her friends can spill their juice and trample in their biscuits and it doesn't matter,' says Lorraine.

This relaxed state of mind also extends to the family's adult visitors and standing on ceremony in the Smith household is strictly forbidden. 'Steve is a far better cook than me and we both enjoy throwing parties but nothing too posh,' Lorraine says. 'I think there's nothing worse on this earth than sitting there in an uncomfortable dress and eating food that's too done up. I prefer to make things simple. To bang it in the middle of the table with plenty of bread and wine and everybody can get stuck in.' She is also happy if most of her parties end up in the kitchen because she says that is one of the most important rooms in any house. 'Ours is tiny but it's cosy. It has a lived-in feel, so it doesn't matter, for instance, if you spill wine on the floor. Whenever anyone has done that in the past it has just kind of got absorbed in the décor. There are worse things in the world than a few wine stains.'

The happy atmosphere got an official seal of approval when Lorraine had a Feng Shui expert round for a slot she was filming for *Nine O'Clock Live*. He says he got good vibes from the start, not least because Lorraine had a bright red front door, which is apparently a perfect welcome. The clutter of toys on the floor, and the walls full of books in almost every room didn't do as well in the Feng Shui stakes, however. But as far as the latter were concerned, Lorraine had no plans to do anything about them. She had loved being surrounded by books in her own childhood and she wanted Rosie to inherit the same passion for reading.

But would she have enough time to inspire her daughter in the years ahead? Like most working mums Lorraine worried endlessly about her new priorities in life. Her own mother had only taken occasional part-time jobs during Lorraine and her brother Graham's childhood, so Lorraine worried that she was doing the wrong thing by effectively working full time. But three things made her feel better about the situation. First was the simple sense that times had changed and that working mothers had become the norm rather than the exception. Second, was the fact that by leaving for work so early in the morning she could still be back in time to spend much of the day with Rosie. Finally, she felt organised enough to make the most of all those precious hours. From the start she decided to mentally earmark specific times of the day to play and chat with Rosie, initially focusing on the hours between tea, bath and bed-time. She carried laminated pictures of her daughter around with her wherever she went, to feel closer to Rosie when they were apart. And she simply tried to deal with the guilt that she is convinced all working mothers feel about their dual roles.

Most of the time the strategy works. But as all parents can attest, it can fall apart in times of crisis. Lorraine and Steve found that out the hard way, just before Rosie's second birthday.

Rosie had been suffering with a nagging cold for some time and was struggling to shake it off. Then, just as she seemed to have recovered and got back to normal, she started to get a temperature. As her tiny body became hotter, she started to shake and jerk as if she were having some sort of awful fit or seizure. Desperately trying to stay calm, Lorraine and Steve tried to remember everything other parents had told them about sudden illnesses. Was this the same? Was it just a fever? Or was it serious? As Lorraine tried to keep Rosie cool and calm, Steve drove them to their local doctor, half of him wanting to break the speed limit to get there fast, half of him aware that this was no time to take any extra risks. After examining the baby, their doctor said she should go to hospital for further tests – immediately. He called an ambulance and the terrified family were rushed across the countryside to hospital. It was the worst time of Lorraine's life.

'I'll never forget the journey to the hospital. Not ever. I thought I was going to lose her. It is at times like those you realise that you would die for your child,' she says, uncharacteristically quiet and with an edge of steely determination in her voice.

After being kept in overnight Rosie soon shook off the virus that had triggered the febrile convulsions and the whole family headed home to recover. Each of them had been through a huge shock. Lorraine and Steve, in particular, had a new sense of perspective about their lives. Family had always come first, for both of them. Now they would ensure this never changed.

For a while, both had been toying with the idea of employing an au pair or a nanny to help them at home – just as many of their local friends had done. Now they decided not to. They knew they could juggle their working lives to share the workload of looking after Rosie, and they wanted to make sure she knew that she was always their key priority. With good friends nearby and Lorraine's parents always happy to head down to Berkshire to help share the load, they were sure they could manage on their own. Anyway, Lorraine had another, much more personal reason for wanting to keep things in the family.

'I want to be able to get up at midnight, naked, and eat ice cream, if I want,' she said with a smile. It was just the kind of relaxed comment she loved to make and it showed just how happy she was in the early spring of 1996. But Lorraine, like everyone else in Britain, was about to get a terrible shock. A tragedy was about to unfold in Scotland and Lorraine was called to the scene within hours. It would cast the darkest of shadows over her for the rest of her life.

9

THE NEWS FROM DUNBLANE

'No one saw it, it wasn't on tape. But I wept and wept.'

It was Wednesday, 13 March 1996 and Lorraine had just got into her car. She was on her way to pick up Rosie from a friend's house and as she flicked on the radio she caught the tail end of what sounded like a newsflash. The words the announcer said seemed to come across in a blur and Lorraine remembers just three of them: 'Shooting', 'School' and 'Scotland'. Horrified and feeling a sudden chill, she pulled over and tried to change channels to hear the news again. When she couldn't, she picked up her phone and rang the GMTV newsdesk.

'"Was I hearing it right?" I asked the staff there, as I told them I reckoned I had misheard the report. It was probably in America, or somewhere else. I probably wanted to believe I had heard it wrongly. But my colleague told me exactly what it was. My stomach felt like ice,' she recalls

The awful story was unfolding in Dunblane, almost halfway between Glasgow and Edinburgh. As we now know, the local loner Thomas Hamilton had burst into the gym of Dunblane Primary School armed with four guns and what would seem like an endless supply of ammunition. The forty-three-year-old fired his first shots at the class teacher Gwen Mayor, who died instantly in front of her terrified children. Hamilton then took aim and killed or injured all but one of the twenty-nine five and six-year-olds in the room. Fifteen of these children died in front of him, one more died after being rushed to hospital for surgery. Hamilton then turned one of his guns on himself and brought the total death toll to eighteen. It was the worst, most evil and most shocking act of violence ever to be carried out in a British school. And as Lorraine tried to focus on the road, the executives at GMTV were getting ready to call her back to London.

Just before midday she and Eamonn Holmes were ushered into the newsroom to be briefed on the latest details of the tragedy. With police cordons still around the school and terrified parents only just finding out what was going on, the information was still sketchy. No one, at this early stage, could quite believe that the worst rumours coming out of the town could be true, but everyone feared they were.

Lorraine, Eamonn and their camera crews were booked on to the first planes to Scotland that the GMTV travel office could find. All remember it as a terrible, terrifying journey, thinking of their own families at home and trying to prepare themselves for the task ahead. For Lorraine it was hard to overcome the disbelief that yet another awful tragedy had hit her beloved Scotland. Piper Alpha, Lockerbie, and now this. And in 1996 she wasn't just a journalist there to report on the story. She was a mother. Dunblane would be a place she would never forget.

The shocks and the horror began the first moment she arrived in the town. While she had been in the air the news had changed fast. In Dunblane, a local policeman was standing in front of the reporters reading out a list of the victims' names. Pulling out her notepad and writing them down as best she could, Lorraine just couldn't believe it. 'I thought, when is he going to stop talking? When will he stop reading the names? He just went on and on. All those poor children's names. The officer found it really hard to speak. I remember thinking how quiet all the journalists were. There was silence. Utter silence. Everyone was white-faced.'

Over the years, Lorraine says she has acquired and even admired the thick skin that many journalists use to inoculate themselves against the horrors of the world they write about; the black humour they use to deflect attention to the shock they might be feeling; the jokes that hide their insecurity or fear. She knows that the siege mentality under which many reporters work can protect them from allowing a story to affect them too deeply. But none of these safety mechanisms were on display in Dunblane. This story was different.

'There wasn't one of us there untouched by pure grief. It was indescribable. I just kept thinking: How can I possibly know what the parents are going through? How can anyone? The atmosphere was different to every other story I have ever covered. I never, not ever, want to feel it again,' she says.

As GMTV prepared to come on air the following morning everyone's challenge was to convey this unbearable atmosphere with respect and dignity. New facts had emerged overnight and the police investigation inside the school would continue for some days. It simply couldn't have been a more sensitive job, balancing the public's need to know with the local population's right to suffer and grieve in silence. Away from the cameras, Lorraine heard stories that will never leave her. Teachers spoke of pupils dying in their arms. Parents described the nightmare of not knowing if their children were alive or dead. And the children themselves spoke of the horrors they had witnessed inside a school that could never be the same again.

With Eamonn at her side, and GMTV's other reporters and staff all around, Lorraine prepared for their first live broadcast. More people watched breakfast television in times of crisis than at any other time. And few events had stunned the country as much as this one. Running through the latest information, speaking to the police and emergency services was hard enough on air. Interviewing local parents was almost too hard to bear. For her part, Lorraine says her biggest challenge was not to lose control and cry on camera. You are reporting on this, you aren't living it, she told herself, echoing her thoughts after Lockerbie and trying to stay strong on their behalf. She did so, but only just.

'On one update I thought, I'm going to cry and there's not a damn thing I can do about it. And I just couldn't hold back the tears. But fortunately the split-second that I broke down was exactly when the bulletin ended and the cameras were off. No one saw it, it wasn't on tape, but I wept and wept. Those poor wee kids and their poor parents and the pain they carry …' Years later, when she finally told the story of the broadcast, her voice tailed off into nothing as she remembered the horrors of those first few mornings in the town.

Lorraine stayed in Scotland for nearly a week of heart-wrenching news reports, interviews and private meetings. She spoke to Steve and Rosie several times every day on her mobile and from her hotel room, and when she finally flew back home she hugged them tighter than she had ever done before. It was the same instinctive reaction of other parents and partners across the country in those low, awful days of March 1996. But as the family tried to settle down again Lorraine's phone rang. Listening to the message in silence she found out that one of the families in Dunblane wanted to talk to her. No one yet knew it, but far from the cameras and in the most awful of circumstances a new and lifelong friendship was about to be born.

* * * * *

Pam and Kenny Ross had lost their five-year-old daughter Joanna in the carnage of the Dunblane gymnasium. After taking their call, Lorraine dropped everything to return to Scotland to spend time with them – though at first she was desperately worried about how she would be received. 'I was humbled they wanted to speak to me and worried about how we had put out the show,' she says. Her worst fear was that there might have been something in one of the tense, live transmissions that had inadvertently upset some of the Dunblane parents. But if so, she was prepared to face up to the mistakes in person and do her best to make amends. It was the most awful situation to be in, and Lorraine admits she had no idea how best to handle it.

A policeman picked her up at the airport. It was only as they were driving to Pam's house that it dawned on her. What would she say? What would she do when she arrived? 'I wasn't a trained counsellor. What if I said the wrong thing? What if I ended up upsetting them even more – if that was possible. I tried to think of how I might feel if it had been my daughter. But I couldn't make that leap because it was so sore. Even now I can't imagine it because it is too painful. The policeman suggested that I just talked. He had had to listen to me on the journey from the airport so by then he realised I could talk.'

It turned out to be the right advice.

'I walked into the house and saw Pam,' Lorraine remembers. 'I don't know what it was but there was an immediate reaction. We just knew we liked each other and I gave her a huge cuddle and she gave me a cuddle. Then we sat and we talked and talked, and I felt as if I had known her for years. From the early stages we just struck it off together and seemed to have a close affinity. We chatted about our families, our backgrounds, and, of course, about the children.'

With the time passing quickly, Lorraine almost forgot that she had some things in her bag which she had planned to give to the Ross family. 'In the panic to get organised I had brought a silver picture frame for Pam so she could put in a picture of Joanna. I knew she had another little girl so I brought along one of Rosie's teddy bears and lots of pictures of Rosie. I didn't even know if it was the right thing to do. I showed her the pictures and I gave her the wee things and she showed me pictures of Joanna.'

It was, Lorraine says, as if she and Pam were in the eye of a storm. Neighbours, friends and family were coming and going all the time and the pair's conversations were constantly being interrupted. But somehow it didn't seem to matter and it didn't appear to break the bond that had already begun to form between them. 'Calm. Very, very calm,' was how Lorraine remembers the atmosphere.

Later, she and Pam were to share an even more moving

moment. Joanne's body had been brought home for a few days before her funeral. After talking late into the night Pam asked if Lorraine wanted to see her. 'I went upstairs and there was this angel lying there in her little Pocahontas nightie, looking perfect. I have never seen a more beautiful child. I howled my eyes out. Pam and Kenny said they would leave me for 10 minutes by myself. Her little bedroom was perfect; a real little girl's bedroom with all her toys and drawings and things around the place. I looked at her and thought, I can't believe there is such evil in the world that would do this to all the children and that lovely teacher.'

Unable to stop her mind racing back to her own child, in her own bedroom hundreds of miles south in England, Lorraine tried to compose herself before facing her hosts again. But there was one more piece of heartbreak to come when Joanne's parents returned. 'Pam asked me to look at the window, and there were little fingerprints on the glass. Can anyone really imagine not being able to clean a window because they didn't want to remove their child's fingerprints?'

* * * * *

A year had passed and while she was often still lost for words at the horror of what had happened in the town, Lorraine agreed to recount her impressions of the tragedy as part of a book, *Dunblane: Our Year of Tears*, all the profits from which went to the Save the Children Fund. She wrote of her friendship with the Ross family. In private, she admitted that while she felt she knew Pam would be a friend for life she will never be able to shake off the ambivalence she feels over the way they had met. 'I wish I had known Pam and Kenny in different circumstances. I wish I had known Joanna. In a way, because of what had to happen before we became friends, I wish we weren't friends and Joanna was still here.'

In October 1996, six months after the tragedy, Lorraine went back to Dunblane for what she described as both a special honour and a huge responsibility. The families of the victims had asked that she read a lesson at the joint memorial service being held in the presence of Prince Charles at Dunblane Cathedral. White candles were to be lit by the families in memory of each of the children, and of their teacher, Gwen Mayor. Lorraine had been asked to read the name of each victim as the candle was lit.

The night before the service a soberly dressed Lorraine was in the cathedral to talk through the order of service with the organiser and other participants. It was a subdued, serious few hours and she was feeling a lot more nervous than she had expected. 'I knew I had to get it right for the children and for their teacher. But I'm not used to reading out loud in large buildings so I had difficulty with that initially. And suddenly the words just wouldn't come out. I was so choked up, I managed to blunder my way through the reading. But when it came to the names at the rehearsal I couldn't do it.'

Not caring a hoot about the cameras, Lorraine was only aware of the grieving parents and relatives who would be in the cathedral the next day. She felt she owed it to them all to find a way through her mental block and she found it with Pam.

'On the morning of the service my nerves were in tatters and I asked Pam if I could go to Joanna's room one more time,' Lorraine says. 'I sat there on her bed, imagining her wee face and all the rest of them. I said: "Right, this is what we're going to have to do – and it's for you." I read it out and got through it without breaking down.'

She believes that had she not done this she would never have managed it in the cathedral. 'To read each victim's name as their families lit a candle was so emotional. I stood there with my fingernails digging into the palm of my hand urging myself to keep control. All I could think about was that this was too important, that I couldn't break down, that it had to be done right. It was difficult for me but God only knows how difficult it must have been for each and every member of the families.

'When I sat down I was beside Mick North, who lost his little girl Sophie, and he gave me a hug and I couldn't even give him a hug back because I thought, if I give him a hug back I'll just start howling. I sat there on the pew, all hunched up, trying to keep myself together.'

As the service continued, the tears would be even harder to stop – especially when the significance of the sixteen small and one large candles was explained. The Very Reverend Professor James Whyte's words were deeply moving, perfectly pitched and utterly correct.

'A candle is small, yet it is a bright, warm light. But the candle is also a symbol of fragility, vulnerability. It is easily snuffed out. Such is our life and the life of the child. Darkness fell on many families and indeed on this entire community on the morning of 13 March. Light was turned into darkness. Yet darkness cannot be allowed to be the last word. Even in the darkest night we may, we must, believe in the light.'

Leaving the cathedral Lorraine gazed directly ahead as she walked into its grounds. She had made several private visits there over the past six months, and would make many more in the years ahead, always bringing freesias for the graves. But that October she couldn't focus on anything. Instead, she could only hear the children's names being repeated again and again in her head. She was still getting flashbacks to her first awful day in the town, when the scale of the tragedy was still unclear. But after hearing the words of the service she too was determined to focus on the light.

Her friendship with Pam would help her to do so. In happier times, in the months ahead, the pair would speak frequently on the phone – sometimes for an hour or more at a time with Lorraine saying it was hard to say exactly which of them was the biggest gas bag. When the Ross family came down to stay with Lorraine, Steve and Rosie, everyone made huge efforts to forget the tragedy that had brought them together. As one big day out in London proved, this wasn't always easy, however. 'On one occasion I could sense that Pam was almost feeling guilty about having enjoyed her day,' Lorraine says. As the pair headed back to Berkshire, she told her she shouldn't feel that way at all. Joanna would have wanted her to have a good time.

* * * * *

The year ended with an unusually muted New Year's Eve – almost the first in her life when Lorraine says she simply didn't have the heart to party or celebrate. After so much tragedy and so many tears she knew it was important to try and set aside as much time as possible for pure, simple fun with Rosie. 'One of the best days we've had recently was when it was pouring with rain. We made chocolate Krispie cakes and also made a right mess. We painted our hands and made handprint pictures, and watched a video and ate so much chocolate we felt sick!' It might not have done much for Lorraine's figure, but it was the perfect start to what she hoped would be a quite different New Year.

10

PRIME TIME

*'Everyone who knows me knows that
I can blether for Britain.'*

Big new doors were opening for Lorraine in the late 1990s
as *Nine O'Clock Live* was relaunched as *Lorraine Live*
and continued to bring in great ratings for GMTV. A steady
stream of production companies got in touch to pitch some
surprisingly big budget programme ideas. Their view was that
by leaving the main *Top Of The Morning* sofa and carving out
a perfect niche after nine, Lorraine had moved on from the
'breakfast ghetto' into the equally attractive daytime market.
The obvious next step, they told her, was prime-time national
television. One hit show and she could be turned into the next
Cilla Black or Chris Tarrant. Lorraine, though, had other ideas.

Fronting up a glitzy evening show just for the sake of it was
anathema to her. She didn't want just to turn up at some
studio, read from an autocue and head off to bank a big
cheque. If she was going to sign up for a new show, she said,
it had to offer her three things: a mental challenge, a sense of
danger and a perfect fit with her childcare arrangements.

So while some entertainment figures were left scratching their heads in bemusement, she was utterly happy with the deal that she did sign up to at the start of 1997. She had said no to all the big budget television shows on offer because she didn't want to work evenings. Instead, she agreed to do a live lunchtime slot on the new and hugely ambitious Talk Radio station. The job fitted in with Rosie's life because the 12–2pm slot meant Lorraine could still be home in time to pick her up from nursery school and spend all afternoon and evening with her, before having an early night so she could get up in time for her breakfast job. Equally importantly, the show offered the intellectual challenge and the sense of danger Lorraine was looking for. The idea was for it to be an entirely different animal to the soft chat of the Radio Two slots she had filled back in 1994. Yes, most of the show would offer easy listening, as Lorraine ran through the news agenda and talked through the latest stories in politics, sport and entertainment.

'Everyone who knows me knows that I can blether for Britain so I am really looking forward to it,' she said of the unscripted part of the show. But in among the chat was an element that promised to be a whole lot more complicated. Lorraine was going to host what *Sunday Times* radio expert Stephen Armstrong called: 'The most ambitious radio phone-in yet.'

The ambition came not in the number of calls she was hoping to attract but in the topics she was putting under investigation. Forget Tony Blair, the Spice Girls or the other obvious stories of 1997. In her first week, Lorraine instead tackled the four different varieties of fascism. The following week the taxi drivers and housewives who made up the bulk of the Talk Radio audience were asked to talk about her take on the theories of French thinker Jean Baudrillard. Academic and Baudrillard expert Chris Horrocks was on the show alongside Lorraine and asked listeners: 'To decide whether Baudrillard is a cure for the vertigo of contemporary culture or one of its symptoms.'

It was heady stuff, as the critics soon realised. 'Now, I don't know if you listen to Talk Radio much, but this isn't the sort of question with which Lorraine Kelly's listeners normally have to deal,' Stephen Armstrong wrote when he reviewed the show. But Lorraine and her producer Dixi Stewart had many more equally tough programmes up their sleeves. Over the next few weeks they researched and ran discussions on Roland Barthes, Jung, postmodernism and Lenin. They wanted to see if listeners cared enough to call in and talk about the psychoanalytic literary critic Jacques Lacan, about Margaret Thatcher, Einstein, Picasso, Keynes, Buddha, ancient and eastern philosophies and, as if all this wasn't broad enough, the nature of the universe.

Lorraine was in her element. She had to do huge amounts of reading each week to prepare for the shows, not least because she didn't want to make a fool of herself when she talked to the experts who joined her in the studio before the phone-ins began. Most amazing of all was the fact that the discussions were a hit. Talk Radio had tested the water by allocating just fifteen minutes of Lorraine's two-hour show to the first debate on fascism. But after that it upped the coverage of the subsequent phone-ins to a full 45 minutes. Critics who said Britain was dumbing down – possibly blaming supposedly lightweight breakfast television presenters for part of the problem – had to eat their words. Lorraine had tapped into a new intellectual well and was thriving.

What made life even better was that the high-brow radio show didn't exclude her from having fun elsewhere – and everyone had fun in two incidents that involved the Spice Girls that summer in 1997. Both happened during the celebrity-studded *An Audience With The Spice Girls*, the kind of show Lorraine rarely took part in but couldn't resist now that the girl band were at the peak of their fabled girl powers. Of all people, 5ft 4in Lorraine ended up doing high kicks with the girls. 'Kicks that went so high that everyone could see I was wearing Marks & Spencer's finest – I am just glad I had put some on!' she remembers, blushing just a little at the memory. Amazingly, her underwear was to get another spice-related showing when she subsequently tried to pull on and walk in a pair of the band's signature platform heels and ended up on the floor à la Naomi Campbell.

Back at Talk Radio two other things were making Lorraine smile every time she arrived at the studios, glasses on and clutching her box files of books and research for that day's show. The first was that her bank balance was doing well – the Talk Radio deal involved a rolling four-year contract that would pay her a total of £1 million if she lasted the course. Nearly a decade before Radios One and Two started paying huge cheques to the likes of Chris Moyles, Jonathan Ross and Chris Evans, this was a near unprecedented payout for a radio presenter and proof of how valuable Lorraine was to the new station.

The other thing that made her smile was that the job hadn't eaten into the time she spent with her daughter. She admits that she had thought long and hard about taking on the lunchtime show. But six months later, Steve confirmed that it had been the right decision.

'He pointed out that I still see more of Rosie than most working mothers so I don't feel I am missing out on her. She is never awake when I get up and I'm usually home just after 3pm in time to spend the rest of the day with her before she goes to bed. I've never had that scenario of my daughter clinging to my leg saying: "Please don't go to work, Mummy". If that ever did happen it would destroy me. Then I would give up work.' Had she done so, then not everyone might have minded. For that summer Lorraine was about to get dragged into a mini-backlash against the so-called 'McMafia' that was dominating the airwaves.

* * * * *

'It begins with Lorraine Kelly bounding on to GMTV in the morning and ends either with Kirsty Wark signing off *Newsnight* at 11.15pm or Lesley Riddoch taking *The Midnight Hour* into the small hours. In between, every day, on television and radio, in the pages of the national press and in the gossip columns, the ubiquity of Scottish women testifies to their recent, and total, conquest of the world,' was how Giles Coren put the domination of Scottish women in *The Times*. Alongside Lorraine, Kirsty and Lesley he pointed to Carol Smiley, Sheena MacDonald, Muriel Gray, Kirsty Young and a host of other behind-the-scenes players, from the new female and Scottish boss of the Royal Opera House to Rhona Cameron of the new and ill-fated Gaytime TV.

Well, Lorraine was certainly not going to apologise for being Scottish – and alongside many of the other women under friendly fire she said her roots made her a better presenter. 'It can be difficult to establish a rapport with a Hollywood star who is doing 110 other interviews on the day you see them,' she said. 'But as soon as they see I am Scottish they always turn out to have an Aunty Fanny in Skye, or be interested in golf or something. Kirk Douglas kept asking me to say things because he liked the accent and Bette Midler grilled me about where to visit when she was in Scotland. It helps you to stand out.'

Channel Five's newscaster Kirsty Young said the Glasgow-based newsrooms where she and Lorraine had both started their careers provided a broadcasting school of hard knocks that was tougher than almost anywhere else in the country. 'What Scottish television makes for itself is news and current affairs programmes, so that is what its graduates are best at,' she said. *Newsnight*'s Kirsty Wark agreed. 'The smallness of BBC Scotland makes the training very rigorous and the lack of money means you have a lot of airtime to fill with unprepared talk. After a few years of that you form some pretty strong opinions.'

This was the training Lorraine had lapped up when she first left the *East Kilbride News* and joined BBC Scotland. It was the discipline she took with her when she moved on to TV-am and then GMTV, covering the Piper Alpha, Lockerbie and Dunblane tragedies. It would put her in good stead for her next set of live outside broadcasts when she went out on to the streets of London on the morning of 6 September 1997 for the funeral of Diana, Princess of Wales.

* * * * *

Diana's death made television stations tear up their ordinary schedules and replace them with rolling news and comment. In the week running up to the funeral, Lorraine's show had almost entirely been taken over by this new agenda and she had struggled, like everyone else, to come to terms with the unfolding events and the unprecedented grief shown across the country.

On the morning of the funeral itself, when she would normally have been at home in Berkshire, she didn't think twice before answering GMTV's call for her to go out on the road with her camera crew. She spoke to Londoners, tourists, people of all ages and backgrounds, coaxing out anecdotes, remembrances and messages. There were tears and there was anger. It was the broadcasting event of everyone's lives, the day millions of viewers would never forget.

Back home, Lorraine could focus only on the human side of the tragedy. She thought of the two boys forced to grow up without their mother and the family torn apart by such an awful accident. As usual, after reporting on tragedies, she hugged her own family a little tighter that night. Seize the day, the mantra she had taken on from her grandmother, seemed more important than ever.

* * * * *

The huge variety of viewers that Lorraine spoke to on GMTV gave her a unique chance to learn about other people's lives. From diets to depression, clothes to confidence she was able to ask questions, listen to experiences and find out more about what makes us all tick. In a nutshell, as she often admits, she has a licence to be nosy for a living.

But talking about viewers' lives only solved one part of her inquisitive nature. As the years went by, she found she was becoming increasingly obsessed by their homes as well.

So in 1998, Lorraine was one of the first television presenters in the country to spot Britain's growing obsession with property. Long before the likes of Sarah Beeny, Phil and Kirsty, Colin and Justin and all the others got on the case, she launched *House Hunters*, which tried to show people how to make the most of their homes. The show was designed to be part quiz, part advice show, and contestants and viewers also had a quick lesson on their local property markets and found out just how they could improve the value of their own properties. 'It also gives us all a super chance to have a good snoop around other people's homes,' she admitted.

But unfortunately for her, the show never really set the world alight. The original series was only shown on Scottish Television at 7.30pm on Thursdays when it was up against the still-strong *EastEnders*. Early reviews were pretty good, but the show never went national or got commissioned for a second series.

So was this the first real failure for Lorraine? In some respects it was, and it proved she still hadn't managed to crack the prime-time evening television market. But the reality was that she was less concerned than many of her television rivals might have been at the early demise of *House Hunters*. She had agreed to make it because it sounded fun and because it fitted in with her schedule. But she hadn't been looking at it as a stepping stone to some bigger production or as a way to generate any extra fame. If people had liked it, then she would have been happy to keep making more shows. As they hadn't, she was happy to carry on with GMTV, Talk Radio and any other one-off productions that might come along. Her aim was never to let work or television take over her life. Her big fear was to get too big for her boots and lose touch with ordinary life.

In May she was to prove that she certainly hadn't done that.

As part of a GMTV special she pulled on a baggy jumper, black trousers and her glasses for a wander around Glasgow's famous Barras market – the place where she and her old school friend Janice had set up their one-day only stall, some two decades earlier.

So much has changed since then, but this place still feels like home, Lorraine thought, wandering around before her camera crew arrived. At this point she simply looked like just another dark-haired mum happily browsing the stalls in search of a bargain or two. But then it began. Someone told her she looked like: 'that Lorraine Kelly woman from the telly'. And when the camera crew turned up, they confirmed it.

'That's Lorraine Kelly. Over there.'

Once word got out it was pandemonium. Lorraine and the crew were scheduled to be on the Barras market for an hour, being filmed for a 'step-back-in-time' slot with GMTV co-presenter and fellow Scot Martin Frizell. But in the end there were so many autograph hunters, and so many people wanting a chat, that Lorraine stayed for nearly three. Even her uncle turned up to say hello, though he preferred to chat to his niece later on at home rather than in the street!

The great thing about that day's filming (Lorraine and the crew retraced several of her other childhood steps after they finally left the market) was that it gave her an extra chance to visit her parents. They were happy to look after Rosie while their daughter filmed and the family had a big get-together with the neighbours in the evening. Always the news girl from East Kilbride, never the big television star from London, Lorraine was happy to muck in, to help with the food and watch Rosie, now four, head off to play with the neighbours' children.

Her next big job was more of a problem, though.

That summer GMTV bosses had decided to film all the 6 to 9.30 slots from Spain for the latest *Fun In The Sun* roadshow. As well as a suite of hotel rooms and apartments, they had booked a massive eighteen-bedroom, £10 million villa in Marbella for the presenters, producers and crew, many of whom would be overseas for up to six weeks. It was the kind of experience Lorraine would have thrived on before Rosie was born, especially as Steve would probably have been on the crew as well. Hitting a few local bars, eating some great food and sleeping in the sun all afternoon all in the name of doing your job seemed a wonderful opportunity for the young, free and single GMTV staff.

But now she was a mother Lorraine wasn't sure she could join in. She was torn between bringing Rosie out for short breaks of a few days a time, having her in Spain for the full six weeks and leaving her at home with her dad. In the end Lorraine and Steve decided that the latter option would probably be the least disruptive and she made sure she would never have to work more than a week without getting a flight back to Britain.

It was, though, the longest time she had been apart from her family so far – and it hurt. She tried not to cry in front of Rosie as Steve drove her to the airport and she managed to hold back the tears as the trio had a final group hug at check-in. Little did she know, as she walked away, that a surprise message was about to leave her in pieces. She was in the line for passport control when she found it. Steve and Rosie had slipped a new photo of the two of them inside her passport along with a message from Rosie saying how much she loved her mum and how much she was going to miss her. 'It was so sweet and I was nearly crying at passport control,' Lorraine says, tempted to turn back and run across the terminal for one last hug.

With her work out of the way, the family did get together for a beach break later that summer. And Lorraine jokes about how much easier holidays are now Rosie is with them. 'Steve is one of those people who has to be doing things all the time and isn't content to just lie on the beach. That's why it is great having Rosie, because now he doesn't bother me,' Lorraine laughs. 'Before he used to lie there for ten minutes and then get up and dig a hole or something. Then I would have to get up and go and look at it and say how great it was. Now I can just leave the two of them together to get on with it.'

The other thing she admits about holidays is that lying on the beach is always a big test of her self-confidence and body image. Some years she is more than happy in her bikini or swimming costume. At other times she feels she has failed her size 12 trousers' test and wants a towel or sarong to pull around her every time she gets up.

What she was about to find out, though, was that she had an unexpected group of fans who couldn't care less about her fluctuating weight – but who were very keen to see pictures of her in her swimwear. At almost forty years old, Lorraine was about to turn into one of the biggest sex symbols on the internet.

11

LORRAINE KELLY: SEX SYMBOL

'They are mad as hatters and seem to be obsessed by my bosom.'

It all began with a letter. In among all her usual mail Lorraine remembers getting a cheeky little note addressed to: 'Dear Lorraine, the woman with the most magnificent bosoms on TV'. She laughed out loud, as she put the letter aside. But soon there was another. And then she realised the messages weren't being sent by a single individual, they were being sent on behalf of a group. A small gang of students had set up The Lorraine Kelly Appreciation Society – and it looked as if they were in it for the long haul.

Old pal and *Daily Mail* writer Lester Middlehurst says the star was just as surprised as everyone else when he first discovered and wrote about the new fan club. This, of course, was a time when the cast of *Friends* were the world's most popular female role models, and when the likes of Melinda Messenger were proving that the allure of a sexy Page Three girl was as strong as ever. 'If one was asked to name the sexiest woman on British television, Lorraine Kelly would not immediately spring to mind,' said Lester – and Lorraine couldn't have agreed more.

But the founder members of the Appreciation Society carried on writing to her. Plenty of light-hearted banter went on by return of post – though after a while the society members seemed to tire of the standard signed photos she was always happy to send them – they wanted some racy shots as well. 'They are mad as hatters and seem to be obsessed by my bosom,' she said, when other reporters followed up the *Daily Mail*'s story and started asking about the group.

For Christmas they sent Lorraine a jar of chocolate body paint, suspenders and stockings with a camera and asked her to pose for some pictures wearing them. 'They know fine well that I won't, but it is rather flattering, albeit hysterical, to think that some people, however mad they are, might think of me in that way,' says Lorraine. 'In the past I have been regarded as "mumsy" and my own mother says she wishes she had a fiver for every time I have been described as "bubbly". So to have a group of young men going on about my cleavage and my legs is interesting to say the least. It's flattering, but I can assure you I don't take it seriously.'

Within a few years, a few other people would be taking it seriously, however. The society had gone online, setting up a website devoted to Lorraine's charms – which in their minds pretty much exclusively meant her breasts. The site itself became something of an online phenomenon, attracting a quarter of a million hits several years before the internet had begun to dominate our work and social lives.

This initial popularity gave the site extraordinary staying power, but it would ultimately draw it to the attention of internet watchdogs. Towards the end of 2003, for example, the regulators objected to some of the computer-enhanced pictures of Lorraine which seemed to have crossed a taste and decency line. Several were not appropriate for a 'non-adult' web address, the regulators said. But after a war of words (both on and offline) the fans said they had won the day and their pictures – less clearly enhanced and cropped to be just a little bit less revealing – remained on the web.

Even then, Lorraine was relaxed enough to see it all as a giant joke. She didn't ever want to take herself too seriously and she refused to get high and mighty over the use of her pictures. She believes that if you earn big money partly because you do your job in the public eye then you can't run to your lawyers every time you see or read something that upsets you. Anyway, when she took a look at the site that had been set up in her name she found it almost impossible not to laugh. 'Wall-to-wall boobies, really. There's boobies, boobies, boobies everywhere! It's bonkers, especially as I don't really go out of my way to show my boobies off – I mean, I just go into shops and buy whatever I like the look of,' she told friends – though she admitted that sometimes her summer wardrobes did leave little to the imagination when she took her jackets off on set.

The next problem for Lorraine, as she tried to cool her fans down, came the rumour that she had in fact stared in a particularly racy photo-shoot. Everyone seemed to know someone who had seen a picture in which she had recreated the famous Christine Keeler pose, sitting apparently naked astride a low-backed chair. For years, Lorraine said the picture would be for her husband's eyes only. But copies did ultimately find their way into the public domain and were soon in pride of place on her fans' websites – and copies of it are now a constant fixture on auction sites like eBay.

As time went on Lorraine also tried to calm things down among her more ardent fans by publicly turning down some of their other suggestions. For example, one day she was posted a silver ankle chain, which the sender desperately wanted her to wear on screen. She never did. Then there were the likes of: 'Dear Lorraine, when are you going to wear something really low cut?' and 'Dear Lorraine, why don't you show off your legs more?' – all diplomatically ignored as well.

'I get the occasional photo of a man's dangly bits but it's usually anonymous and goes straight in the bin,' she says, of her postbag. As far as she is concerned, the less said the better about the red leather knickers and black leather whip that arrived out of the blue one morning and caused more than a little concern at the GMTV offices.

Security sources say that Lorraine treats her racier fans in exactly the right way. 'Everyone in the public eye, and women in particular, do need to pay attention to the way they are perceived, and there can be a fine line between a healthy, amusing interest and an unhealthy, very unsavoury obsession,' says consultant Mark Elliott, who has looked after the security of dozens of big-name actors and presenters since leaving the army in 1994. 'The way you treat the first few letters or communications from any given fan can set the boundaries for everything that will follow. Being too defensive can cause problems, as can being too relaxed. One good way to diffuse any situation is to use humour, though you need to make it clear you are laughing with your fans rather than at them.'

Lorraine has never had any problem laughing at herself so she managed to walk the line successfully in all her dealings with fans. She is proud of the way she can empathise with and understand other people, and reckons she has an in-built sensor for trouble. Having interviewed victims of stalkers as both a newspaper and television reporter has also kept her on her toes. She never forgets that the world can be a dangerous place and is constantly on her guard against anything that could affect her or her family's equilibrium.

* * * * *

In 1998, it wasn't just heterosexual men who were demanding ever more attention from Lorraine, however. She had been steadily building up a huge fan base among gay men as well, so when a group of them asked for a very special photo shoot she was ready to oblige.

The role in question was as cover star for *Boyz* magazine, a free title handed out in pubs and clubs in London. Big name celebrities such as Texas singer Sharleen Spiteri had just done shoots for the magazine and its chief photographer Mark Flaherty says they were determined to make Lorraine their latest hot Scot on the cover. 'She was at the very top of our hit list when we decided on new people to feature because she is so cool and very, very sexy,' says Mark. But would she agree? The editor approached Lorraine's manager and prepared for a tough negotiation. But they didn't get one. Lorraine said yes straight away.

'I really didn't have to be persuaded,' she says. 'I just thought: Why not? The whole thing was hilarious. Normally I hate getting my photograph taken but that was one of the nicest photo sessions I have done, with a wind machine, the whole thing. I'm just glad I seem to scrub up well when I get the right help. The clothes were fabulous as well, all made by young Scottish designers which made it even better.'

Mark says Lorraine turned out to be 'a dream model' and was clearly up for a laugh from the very start. The magazine had come up with a huge range of clothes and props, including a golden tiara, a chocolate brown stole, lots of fake fur and feathers. No one knew if she would be prepared to send herself up by wearing them, but everyone loved it when she was.

With the shoot over and all the best shots selected for the magazine Lorraine tried to find out why the staff had been so keen to put her on their cover. 'They said it was because my show is quite camp and because I make lots of little bitchy remarks which I wasn't really aware of. When we're doing a fashion item they say I always arch my eyebrows and say: "But how does it relate to the high street?" That's my gay catchphrase, apparently. I suppose GMTV in general is really popular with gay men because we do such daft things in the name of entertainment. And I think it is wonderful, a real compliment, to have so many gay fans.'

For their part, the *Boyz* staff said Lorraine was a joy to work with – and someone British broadcasting could ill afford to lose. 'To us Lorraine is like a real-life Teletubby,' said one of the magazine writers. 'That's nothing to do with what she looks like. It's just that when she is on TV you know nothing awful can happen in the world and that's what we love most about her.'

Up in East Kilbride Lorraine's mum laughed away when she heard about the photo shoot and the ridiculous poses she had struck. And just as she still tried to watch every show her daughter appeared in, she wanted to buy every magazine that featured her. Getting hold of *Boyz*, however, was a bit of a challenge, as Lorraine remembers. 'My mum and my Aunt

Josephine went looking for *Boyz* in WH Smith in Glasgow, only to be politely told that newsagents don't stock magazines for hardcore gay clubbers.' Not to be deterred, Anne and Aunt Josephine demanded their own copy be posted up to them – even after Lorraine had warned them a little more about what to expect on the other pages. The website her fans had set up about her might have been wall-to-wall boobies, as she had said earlier. This magazine was wall-to-wall something else. 'What a laugh it was – because the magazine is just full of willies. It's just willies galore! Willies everywhere! Ginormous willies!' she laughed, as she leafed through it and then posted a copy up to Scotland, desperately hoping it wouldn't offend.

'Dear Lorraine, how dare you have a photograph of your naked bottom put on posters? You should know better and you should be ashamed of yourself.' Sitting in her office at home in Berkshire, Lorraine read the letter several times. She hadn't offended her mother or her aunt with the *Boyz* magazine. But it seemed she had somehow upset someone else. But what on earth was this lady talking about? Lorraine asked around and when she found out, for a split second she almost lost her legendary sense of humour.

She had known that a new advertising campaign for the latest series of her Talk Radio show was being launched on billboards across the country. What she hadn't realised was that some of the first posters were eye-catching, to say the least. The first of them showed a woman's bare bottom stamped with a bar code – the idea was to promote Lorraine's first discussion programme about prostitution. 'It is embarrassing and the first I knew about it was when I got the letter of complaint from an angry lady. Now I just want to reassure people that it's not my bottom on the posters. And I'm also worried that listeners and viewers will think I talk out of my bottom,' she quipped, as that week's show ended, a new set of posters went up around the country and her sense of humour returned.

Others would be taking the image a bit more seriously for a while longer, however. The Advertising Standards Authority (ASA) was asked to investigate the posters on taste and decency grounds while the AA said drivers could be distracted by them – just as many had been by the iconic Eva Herzigova 'Hello Boys' posters of the previous year.

* * * * *

Back in the world of work, after nearly two long and successful years in the Talk Radio hot seat, Lorraine was ready to take advantage of the break clauses in her contract and move on. The Talk Radio show had gone well, with Lorraine controlling a surprisingly heated set of studio guests and reigning in some of her more opinionated callers, and it was a wrench. She loved the show, the production staff and the whole challenge of covering unexpectedly complicated subjects for a live audience. But the hours were proving harder to cope with than she had expected. Traffic seemed to be getting worse and she wasn't always able to pick Rosie up from school at 3pm any more. Privately she also told friends that she felt as if she no longer had any time to herself – and the time she did have was taken up reading up for her next programme. More worryingly she had once more dramatically started to fail her size 12 trousers test. While she certainly didn't want to go shopping to find out the worst, her best guess was that she would need to go back to the size 16 rack in most high street stores. Something had to be done.

'I felt I was getting very unfit and fat, and that leaving the show was the only way I could do anything about it,' she says. Having done so, she vowed to make the most of the time she was saving. She threw herself back into village life in Berkshire, pitching in at birthday parties for Rosie's friends and starting a new DIY blitz on the family home.

She also wanted to kickstart her life with a new exercise campaign – and she thought she knew just the woman to help her. Ex-gymnast and now fitness and nutrition expert Jenni Rivett had been a personal trainer to the late Princess Diana as well as scores of other high profile clients. Jenni's belief – explained in her *Jenergy* books – was that women needed specially tailored advice to reflect their body shapes and lifestyles. Lorraine and Jenni met up, hit it off and started a six-week body-busting campaign. The pair worked out in Lorraine's house and at a local gym, and the results soon started to show. GMTV staff and viewers all began to comment on how good she was looking, and after a couple of months she headed out to dinner with Steve wearing a pair of her lucky size 12 trousers. She was feeling on top of the world. But was the world ready to find out how she had done it? Could thirty-nine-year-old Lorraine Kelly, of all people, join the ranks of the young, super-fit and normally wafer-thin stars who produced fitness videos?

The bosses of one big production company thought that she could. They got in touch when news of her link up with Jenni first broke and argued that Lorraine's 'everywoman' credentials as a working mother who struggled with her weight just like everyone else made her a perfect role model. But Lorraine still needed persuading. Wouldn't people mock her for setting herself up as some kind of body beautiful? And what if the tape flopped?

In the end, two things persuaded Lorraine to go ahead. First, she couldn't argue that the routines she had been given by Jenni worked, so it seemed only fair to help promote them to others. And also, she realised that being laughed at had hardly bothered her in the past, so wasn't going to stop her taking on a new challenge now.

She and Jenni got together to work on a script and a shooting schedule and then went into the studio to start filming. The result, *Figure It Out With Lorraine Kelly*, turned into the surprise bestseller of the Christmas and New Year season. It hit the Number 2 slot in the overall video sales charts after selling 60,000 copies in its first three weeks of release. The producers, Polygram, were staggered. 'We can't believe the success and we are having to rush out more copies now because of the demand,' said a spokesman. Fellow breakfast television presenters who had their own fitness videos on release, including Anthea Turner and Astrid Longhurst, were being easily outsold by their more mature colleague.

Asked why she thought her tape was doing so well, Lorraine kept it simple. 'It's very down to earth and very do-able,' she said. 'I'm not a supermodel, after all, but a mum. So it is something other mums can easily fit into their lives in between doing the housework and looking after the kids. I used to buy exercise videos by the likes of Cindy Crawford and Cher, but women who look like that are born that way. I'm never going to look like them. But this exercise programme really works and I'm absolutely delighted at how popular it is.'

Over the next few years, exercise would become increasingly important in Lorraine's life. It gave her a huge new interest, a fresh challenge and the chance to raise hundreds of thousands of pounds for charity. So all those who criticised her first fitness tape as a cynical bid to jump on a bandwagon and earn a bit of extra cash would have to eat their words.

Exercise also helped her to free her mind from worries about food. The more she and Jenni talked about fitness campaigns, the more Lorraine realised that this, rather than dieting, was the way to get the body shape she had always wanted. Now, if she wanted to sit down one Saturday night and eat a whole bag of bite-sized Mars Bars while watching a black-and-white Bette Davis movie then she could do so. On GMTV she became increasingly vocal on the subject, no longer enjoying the traditional discussions of the latest 'miracle diets' that promised so much but never seemed to deliver. 'Diets make food so much more important than it should be,' she said after yet another theory was expounded on the show. 'Because of that you find yourself going to bed at night thinking about what you are going to have for breakfast the next morning and fantasising about cornflakes, which is terribly sad. Basically, if you are hungry then eat. Don't sit there with your face ricocheting off the floor while the rest of your family are enjoying a curry! Have a little bit of what they are eating and if you keep up with your exercises, you'll be fine.'

As usual, she could never be accused of patronising her fans with these kind of opinions because she had so obviously lived through all the same issues as her viewers. 'I've been on every diet going over the years, proper ones and faddy ones. I reckon that since I was a teenager I must have gained and lost the equivalent weight of three large rugby players,' she said, only half-joking. The effects, she added ruefully, have not always been pleasant. 'I used to overdo diets so that all they ever resulted in was chronic constipation (the hard-boiled egg diet) and a life-long aversion to citrus fruits (the grapefruit diet). I won't even go into the consequences of the high-fibre bran diet,' she jokes.

As proof of how much good her alternative exercise regime had done, Lorraine went out clubbing in February 1999 – and nearly ended up dancing till dawn. She joined a bunch of other friends and famous names at the final night of the Love Muscle gay night at the Fridge nightclub in Brixton, south London. Almost all of them left just before midnight, just as Lorraine had done when she and her pals had gone to clubs back in Glasgow and she needed to be ready for an early shift at the BBC or TV-am. A decade on and she wanted to let her hair down and forget work responsibilities for a while. So she went on stage for some banter with the club's resident drag queen Yvette, headed back to the dance floor and then didn't leave the club till the doors closed just after 3.30am.

* * * * *

One reason for the rare night on the tiles was that Lorraine knew her workload was about to get a lot tougher. Free time would once more be at a premium as she went back to her reporter's roots. She was unveiled as the new star columnist in *The Sun* with a full page to fill every Monday, writing under the banner: 'Real views, from a real woman'. The difference between Lorraine and many of the other famous names who had their photo at the top of a comment page was that she planned to write every word herself.

Several columnists have been renowned in the industry for just supplying a few basic topics they would like to cover and letting some anonymous staff writer turn them into sparkling prose. Others do even less, allowing the staff writers to choose the subjects, write them up and have them printed without the celebrity even taking a look. 'The only time she ever picked up a pen was to sign the contract,' is a typical comment from one so-called ghost-writer who did all the hard work for a celebrity columnist without getting either the credit or the financial rewards.

Lorraine swore that no one would ever have cause to make comments like this about her. She put aside specific times in her week to focus on the research and writing and says she could often be found at her desk hours after Rosie had gone to bed and while Steve was watching television in the next room. She thrived on the challenge.

Her brief at *The Sun* was to be controversial, opinionated and funny. She could write about any current event, from news and sports to celebrity or entertainment stories. It was her perfect job and she was determined to be as successful at it as the doyennes of the genre, the late Jean Rook and Lynda Lee-Potter who she had read avidly as a reporter on the *East Kilbride News*. After less than four weeks, *The Sun* was ready to confirm that she was a hit. Every newspaper's postbag is widely seen as the best indication of how well individual columnists are doing. The letters that come in don't all have to be positive – a huge stack of post angrily disagreeing with a writer is seen as far better than just one letter of quiet approval. The point is to make waves – and Lorraine was splashing around for all she was worth.

Her editors said she had an uncanny knack of knowing which stories were at the forefront of readers' minds. She wrote things the way she saw them – the Lorraine Kelly who could talk unscripted on radio or on television for as long as her producers required was able to fill just as much space on the page.

That summer, her reputation for straight-talking was to take a hit in the television studios, however. Unknown to her, she was about to be dragged into the so-called 'bogus guest' crisis that had gripped the daytime television market. Vanessa Feltz and Trisha Goddard had both been under fire for inadvertently having actors rather than members of the public as guests on their shows.

Then, without Lorraine's knowledge, it turned out that the lady who came on to her show to talk about having had £4,000 of hi-tech fat removal treatment with a cosmetic surgery group was nowhere near as independent as she looked. A viewer rang in to say she thought the guest was actually an employee of the clinic being discussed, but by the time this was confirmed the show was over and the damage done. Station chiefs launched an investigation into what was a clear breach of the show's rules. Hugely aware of the importance of trust, Lorraine was mortified. Having been a television researcher herself in the past, she knew just how much pressure these lowly paid staff were under to book guests for each show and part of her sympathised with what could have been a genuine mistake. But appearances mattered on her show, and she knew they all had to prove that this was an unfortunate yet unforgivable error that would never be repeated.

* * * * *

Any anger she felt over the scandal was easy to work off because she had begun yet another new exercise campaign and was in the process of filming her second fitness video. Last time around, the key message of the tape was that Lorraine had lost a stone in six weeks. But, like everyone else who loses weight, the real challenge had been in keeping it off – and this seemed to be the ideal focus for a follow-up production.

Lorraine Kelly's Figure Happy was being prepared for a launch in December 1999 with a simple message on the video and DVD cover: 'I'm still a stone lighter – more than a year later', with Lorraine proving it as she stretched out in a black leotard and white training shoes.

Filming this second video had been even more fun than the first. By now, she and Jenni were even better friends and utterly comfortable in each other's company. Knowing that the first tape had been a bestseller made the rest of the crew equally relaxed, so the four days of filming sometimes felt more like a holiday than hard work. The photo shoot for the cover was equally fun, because Lorraine was finally starting to relax in front of the cameras. Unlike many famous faces she says she has never really enjoyed being photographed and reckons she looks strained and nervous in many of her school pictures and even family holiday shots. But as the years went by and she became more content with her body and her image, she was finally able to let go. The cover shots for *Boyz* magazine had been a big step – proving that if she relaxed totally and focused on having fun the pictures could take care of themselves. Since then, her publicity shots for GMTV showed a more confident, professional-looking Lorraine, finally at ease as the centre of attention.

At the end of November 1999, a final set of pictures were to show that the transformation from a shy schoolgirl and an uncomfortable young woman into a surprisingly self-assured beauty was complete. It was Lorraine's fortieth birthday, and she wanted to pass the milestone on a high.

12

FABULOUS AT FORTY

'Perhaps there is a new me bursting forth.'

Lorraine slipped on the pink, Karen Millen leather jacket and took a long hard look at herself in the mirror. She could easily afford it – but should she buy it? The more she looked at the jacket the more she worried. It seemed too frivolous, too risky, too unlikely to work with anything else in her wardrobe. But it was fun – and for once she decided to throw caution to the wind and go for it.

'It was my birthday present to myself,' she told her friends when she got home, still not quite sure why she felt the need to justify both the money she had spent and the style of the jacket itself. Talking it over with the fashion and style experts at the studio, she decided she should make more impulse buys like this if she wanted to avoid being pigeon-holed as a mumsy, mainstream television presenter. 'I'm not over the hill yet,' she told her team, after doing a feature on celebrity women in their 50s and 60s who all looked as sparkling and sexy as they had done several decades earlier.

As if to prove her point, Lorraine gave herself another little fortieth birthday gift. She agreed to pose for *Hello!* magazine wearing her new pink jacket and any of the other clothes the stylists thought she should try. It would be her chance to shine, and she planned to dazzle.

Before the shoot, Lorraine joined the magazine staff to talk about the kind of look she was hoping to project – she pointed to some recent pictures of fifty-something star Lulu, who she reckoned could pass for a teenager. She also told the stylists that her dream was to look like Vivien Leigh, but her nightmare was that in fact her round face made her look more like her father back in East Kilbride.

Gary Cockerill, the top make-up artist, who amazingly enough had once been a Yorkshire coal miner, was quick to put Lorraine at her ease. He says he liked her, from the moment that he met her at the studio, and that when he likes a subject he tends to get the best out of them. His recent work with Barbara Windsor and Caprice had been widely praised and Lorraine says she decided to surrender to him completely. For her part, she admits that she had much to learn from him because she hadn't changed her make-up routine in years. 'When I am on set the staff put together the certain breakfast television look that we pretty much have to stick to and when I'm not at work I don't wear very much make-up at all,' she admits. 'I seem to have inherited my mother's good skin and my make-up bag is normally filled with a few old faithfuls that last forever. For this shoot it was nice to put myself in the hands of the professionals and just let them work their magic. Perhaps there is a new me bursting forth,' she said.

Gary and the rest of the team helped Lorraine have fun, with a Geisha look and a Judy Garland being judged the most eye-catching and successful. The forty-year-old could still turn heads and switch on some old-fashioned Hollywood glamour when required.

* * * * *

The week after the shoot Lorraine had to put on the Ritz one more time as her show was being broadcast live from a tinsel-laden Leeds Castle in Kent as part of GMTV's pre-Christmas line-up. These kind of outside broadcasts could be both great fun and hugely stressful. Having spent most of the year working in the annexe of the former LWT Tower on the south bank of the River Thames, most of the staff were ready for a change. But the technicians in particular say a lot more work has to be done in a new venue than meets the eye. And a lot of things can go wrong when the red transmission lights go on.

For Lorraine, getting out on the road always feels a bit like getting back to her reporter's roots, and as long as they're not too far from home she thrives on GMTV's occasional away-days and weeks. The only problem with this one, as all her colleagues agreed, was that the extra-long commute made it a little bit harder for everyone to organise their own Christmas holidays. In Berkshire, Lorraine's to-do list was even longer than normal because her mum and dad were both heading south to join them, along with Steve's sister. Lorraine was also approaching the end of her first stint on the Parent Teacher Association at Rosie's school and had agreed to help out at the Christmas concert by organising goody bags for all the children. With her brother spending the holiday in Singapore and most of her other relatives still in Scotland, she had to keep an eye on the last posting dates for parcels and swooped on Fortnum & Mason on London's Piccadilly to organise typically British hampers for all of them.

She and Steve also had a fun time going out to buy a Christmas tree, which was about to get a very special decoration – 'Rosie made a Christmas fairy at school and you have never seen such a sorry state. But I wouldn't put anything else on top of my tree,' said the proud mum. She has always been a huge fan of Christmas, saving special decorations year after year and enjoying the sense of history and family heritage they produce each time they come down from the attic. Tartan ribbons, of course, are particularly well represented among the other bells and baubles.

On Christmas Eve itself a desperately excited Rosie was finally persuaded to go to sleep after leaving out the traditional glass of whisky for Father Christmas and a carrot for Rudolf. With the whisky all drunk and the carrot half eaten, Lorraine then nailed a piece of red fabric inside the chimney as proof that Santa had been to visit and had accidentally snagged his trousers on the way back to his sleigh. The following day everyone was up early to open their presents and Steve was soon locked away in the kitchen preparing his traditional Christmas lunch. Afterwards, Lorraine had just one more family tradition to relive. She joined her dad in the kitchen and they did the washing up – just as they had always done three decades earlier in East Kilbride.

* * * * *

After her own low-key fortieth birthday celebrations in November of the previous year, Lorraine was ready to up the ante when her best pal Joyce passed the same milestone in

January 2000. The pair had decided to go on a girls-only, shop-till-you-drop trip to New York. When they booked the holiday they were amazed at how cheap the tickets were, putting it down to the fact that as most people have probably been overspending over the Christmas period the travel companies know holidaymakers will be thin on the ground in January. But as soon as they left JFK and headed towards the taxi rank the pair realised there was another reason: it was absolutely freezing cold. 'Three years ago, I took Rosie to Lapland to meet Santa in the Arctic Circle but it was nothing compared to January in New York,' says Lorraine. 'I've never been so cold in my life! We had to get hats and coats that looked like cast-offs from Liberace. There we were, trying to be all glam, but so muffled up we could hardly see out or be seen.'

As two proud Scotswomen, the cold wasn't going to stop them having fun, especially as they were on a mission. The New York sales had just begun and both Lorraine and Joyce had brought empty suitcases with them that they intended to return home full to the brim. Their first stop, they decided, would be Fifth Avenue, closely followed by Bloomingdales, Barneys and all the other classic New York department stores. But first they popped down to the hotel bar for a quick drink – which soon turned into two and nearly spelt disaster. 'To warm ourselves up and get in the New York state of mind we had martinis, which over there are pure gin with a twist of lemon,' remembers Lorraine. 'Two of them and we were away! We staggered down Fifth Avenue and went into the famous Saks store. A make-up girl absolutely plastered us with make-up and stung us for a hundred dollars. The look was scary, too much for both of us.'

Fortunately they were ready to laugh at each other's new New York looks in the Saks ladies room and then the shopping finally got started.

The following day, with their suitcases half-full, the pair took a break for some sightseeing. They decided to go on a helicopter trip around the Statue of Liberty and up the Hudson River. But they didn't just find any old helicopter pilot. 'Ours turned out to be a Vietnam vet and it was a thrill ride. We went round the Statue of Liberty so fast it was like a blur,' Joyce remembers. Back in their hotel, the pair also sat and laughed along at some of the worst American television – and more importantly, the worst American commercials – that they could find.

It had been a brilliant start to the year, and as they flew back to Britain Lorraine and Joyce were both feeling euphoric about the way their friendship had lasted and how good their lives had become. Both were hugely grateful that their relationship had seen them through so many years and so many ups and downs – in three years' time, they decided, they should head back to New York for a follow-up trip to celebrate three decades of their extraordinary friendship.

* * * * *

Before then, Lorraine had plenty of extra work to do at the GMTV studios. *Lorraine Live* was being given a big revamp in 2000, and a new name – *LK Live*. However, within a matter of days of the new-look show coming on air, she thought it might be doomed. The near disaster came when a guest for a fashion slot almost put a pair of shoes on the coffee table in front of her. A look of total panic flashed across Lorraine's face as she stopped what she was saying and leant across to grab her guest's arm. Not putting shoes on a table is just one of the superstitions she can't say she really believes in – but can't quite bring herself to dismiss either. She won't walk under ladders and says she is constantly throwing salt over her shoulders at home.

With the shoes firmly placed on the floor and the show's good karma retained, the new format was given a chance to bed down. But while viewers were happy and the ratings stayed high, the critics were expected to be a lot harder to please. Lorraine's success had made her an obvious target for anyone wanting to score cheap points by criticising popular culture. It turned out that while several critics didn't like the structure or even the content of *LK Live* they could hardly fault its host.

Tom Lappin, a television critic who has followed Lorraine Kelly's career closely over the years, made the point most effectively. 'The show is an awkward blend of lifestyle, current affairs, "issues" and trivia that could make alarming cranking noises as the disparate elements crash together,' he wrote in the *Sunday Times*. 'But with the reassuring lubrication of Kelly's presence it all makes a kind of sense. You need a peculiar and a particular talent to whip the fluffy and the serious into a show that is neither excruciating nor embarrassing. It's a talent possessed by Lorraine and only a handful of her peers in broadcasting,' he concluded.

What the critics were starting admit was that breakfast and daytime television is a lot harder to make than it looks – especially when it is broadcast live. Tabloid newspaper journalists have long since worked under the belief that 'easy reading is hard writing'. Finally, it was becoming clear that it was the same for television. Just because Lorraine made it look easy, it didn't mean that it was something anyone could do. Knowing she was good at her job gave her a huge amount of quiet confidence and allowed her to brush off the occasional criticism she attracted. It also meant that she never lost her ability to laugh at herself – as she proved a few months later when she was in London hosting GMTV's live coverage of the year's Oscars.

'Michael Caine had just won his Best Supporting Actor Oscar for *The Cider House Rules*. He was clutching his award and getting ready for some interviews when the GMTV people grabbed him and told him he was live on British television talking to Lorraine Kelly. He looked thoroughly underwhelmed and his first two words on live television were: "Who's she?" The whole studio was laughing – and I couldn't help joining them,' she says.

Other unexpected surprises that summer showed just how capable she was of keeping control when things went wrong during a live broadcast. A new wave of rivalry between GMTV and Channel 4's *Big Breakfast* had erupted. At its peak *Big Breakfast*'s Richard Bacon arranged for a streaker to run across the screen during a live link between Lorraine in London and the Cannes film festival in France. The man – an Australian stripper who was wearing a G-string with strips of bacon on it – ran behind reporter Jackie Brambles halfway through her report.

'Don't look at that man!' screeched Lorraine at her colleague, who was blissfully unaware of what was going on behind her. Lorraine, as usual, had the last clever word. 'Everything was a long way away but there didn't seem to be much to get excited about. It must have been very cold out there,' she pronounced, in the ultimate put down.

For all the success she was enjoying on screen, however colleagues admit that her off-screen world was nowhere near as glamorous as many viewers might have thought. In his autobiography *This Is My Life*, co-host Eamonn Holmes said there was no room for luxury behind the scenes at GMTV – especially for the female presenters. 'If the boys were cosy, the girls were positively claustrophobic,' he said of the dressing room situation – with Lorraine sharing a tiny cubicle with Penny Smith, and all the other presenters crammed into even smaller spaces alongside them. Funnily enough, Lorraine and Eamonn were still seen as one of the country's most popular breakfast double acts, even though they hadn't shared the sofa on a regular basis for some time. They were not, however, immune from the usual insults from the press. When she assessed all the major breakfast television partnerships for a *Sunday Times* profile that year, Rachel Cooke didn't spare GMTV's big names. Lorraine and Eamonn were given just ten out of twenty in the 'Looks' category, where they were dismissed with the single line: 'Both are moon-faced and squat'.

They were awarded the same score for 'Sexual Chemistry', with the comment: 'It is hard to believe that they are capable of doing it with anyone, let alone each other.' After a series of other categories the pair were also awarded a low score under 'Intellectual Depth', where Cooke concluded: 'Put it this way: interviewing a *Home and Away* star is considered a challenge on GMTV'. That said, when the spoof 'Dream Dishes at Breakfast' awards were handed out, Lorraine and Eamonn's total score of sixty eight out of a hundred edged them ahead of Richard and Judy, although they were well behind the poll-winning combination of Chris Evans and Gaby Roslin.

On her current show, Lorraine was still enthusing like crazy about the latest fashions, make-up tips, celebrity gossip or travel ideas. Contrary to some cynical expectations, her constant enthusiasm was genuine. 'The Lorraine you find in her grubby dressing room half an hour after her live show is pretty much the same as the Lorraine chatting to guests on camera,' says journalist Tom Lappin, who was following up his review of her show by watching Lorraine from the wings all day in a bid to pin down the secrets of her success.

Something he also spotted was that she acts in exactly the same manner to her celebrity guests as to non-celebrities, working particularly hard to put the latter at their ease. 'With the public I always make a point of meeting the guests beforehand, of getting to know them a little,' she told him, when he mentioned it. The previous week, for example, a member of the public was due on the show to talk about the extraordinary twenty stone she had lost by sensible dieting. 'She was very nervous about going in front of the camera,' says Lorraine. 'But very early on in the morning I met her in the loo – I had my curlers in – and she was fine as soon as we started chatting. You could see the nerves disappearing and she made a brilliant guest when the show finally began.'

Lorraine's kindness towards the general public wasn't confined to those appearing on her show, however. It was just after Tom had shadowed her for the day that the *News of the World* decided to resurrect an old chestnut of an investigation into the behaviour of Britain's biggest stars. Reporters pulled together a list of famous names and sent them all letters from a fictitious eight-year-old fan they called Ben. They asked for a signed photo, some tips on how to become famous and sat back to see if any of the celebrities would bother to reply.

Under the headline 'Lorraine's A Bit Of All Write' the paper announced that she topped the survey as the fastest and the kindest of the big names in its mini-survey. As well as the signed photo, Lorraine had sent a handwritten note suggesting Ben wrote to his local papers and radio stations, and tried to do some work experience there when he was older. 'Good luck, love Lorraine,' she wrote at the end.

It was far more than the vast majority of other celebrities had found the time to do. Most had not responded at all, the paper said, and those who did often just sent unsigned photos, pictures with pre-printed signatures and no individual responses. Lorraine says that kind of high-handed behaviour wasn't something she could ever consider – she still felt hugely grateful for the support she got from her fans and didn't want any of them to think they were being taken for granted. 'If people take the time to write, the least I can do is reply,' she told *News of the World* reporter Douglas Wight when he called to tell her she had topped the paper's poll and that 'Ben' didn't really exist. 'I wrote to stars when I was young and it was great when they got back to me.'

Faced with such a kind and generous public image, the GMTV producers and writers found they could still come in for a shock behind the scenes, however. For Lorraine admits that when it comes to certain subjects she can be a lot tougher than she looks. The big issue, she says, is almost always the same: Scotland.

'I am always fighting for the Scottish dimension,' she says of the most regular production battles at GMTV. She frequently complains when there are stories about heatwaves in England and people are shivering north of the border, for example. On screen she is not averse to some light-hearted teasing on the subject either. 'What makes me laugh is when I'm doing an interview with some big American star. They will say they're touring England, and I'll pick them up and say: "Really? Your tour schedule says you're playing in Aberdeen. Have you cancelled that then?" That really confuses them.'

When she is trying to wind up her English colleagues or Berkshire neighbours she has plenty of other favourite lines to offer. 'My favourite view? The ground from the aeroplane as I'm about to land in Glasgow. My heart leaps,' she says with a smile. Equal favourite, she continues, is the 'Welcome to Scotland' sign she sees when she crosses the border by car. 'Like every Scot, I cheer my head off. It's not an insult, honest – it's just that I feel like I'm home once I've seen it.'

When she is day-dreaming, Lorraine has an idea that she thinks would make even more of a statement on the road – she once saw a blue car with a Scottish flag on the roof and has wondered ever since if it might be possible to find a fully tartan car. 'Maybe I could customise a Smart car,' she mused with friends, after coming back from a holiday in Rome, where she saw the tiny motors for the first time and fell in love with them.

Scots also score highly in her mental list of the world's most attractive men. Loyal as ever, she puts husband Steve in pole position, closely followed by Glasgow-born Gordon Ramsay. Next, she confesses to a long-standing crush on Gordon Brown (possibly on the back of which she managed to persuade him to come on the show and help man the phone lines during a charity telethon). One Frenchman makes it into her all-time top five – Gérard Depardieu. And then one man who is, quite literally, from another planet. 'I have got a strange taste in men. One of my all-time favourites is Mr

Spock from *Star Trek*. Not Leonard Nimoy himself, but the character. He has hidden emotion so being with him would be an incredible challenge.'

Back on earth, and having met and interviewed so many of the most attractive people of both sexes, Lorraine reckons she knows exactly what she does and doesn't like. 'It has to be the rugged men for me. The pretty boys tend to be dull. Brad Pitt is beautiful but leaves me cold.' George Clooney, she is happy to admit, has the exact opposite effect.

13

TRAGEDY

*'Having Rosie meant I couldn't wallow in misery.
I couldn't go to my bed and cry all the time, much as
I wanted to, because I had to think of her.'*

Lorraine closed her eyes and sat back in the car as she was driven west after filming *LK Today*. Her face was fresh and make-up free, and, as usual, she had taken out her contact lenses in the dressing room and pulled on a pair of glasses immediately after the show. She was tired, but she was smiling to herself as the car drifted through the late-morning traffic. For once, she didn't have any other work lined up for that day. She was on her way home and she was looking forward to catching up with her daughter.

It was 2000, and Rosie, far from the public eye, was growing up into a confident, well-adjusted and happy little soul. All of Lorraine's fears over not being able to be there when she woke up had come to nothing. Steve was happy to take over most of the morning duties, sharing breakfast with his daughter and taking her to school most days. Lorraine loved taking over the responsibilities as early as her daily workload allowed. When she got home she normally stood quietly for a while watching Rosie play or eat, or carry on with whatever task she was working on. Then she waited for the wave and the smile that mum gets as a thank you for coming home.

'I'd love her to run up and hug me when I come home, but she usually just looks up and says: "Hi". She's a very self-sufficient, contented little girl,' Lorraine said, too honest to lie and suggest the Kelly household is the scene of some emotionally charged, Hollywood-style reunion five days a week. 'Even at four she was four going on forty, and she does seem to understand that I need to go to work but that I'll always be back soon.'

It adds up to a calm, relaxed atmosphere in a very happy home. Looking back, Lorraine was hugely grateful that she had decided to turn down the various prime-time shows she had been offered over the past few years. Sticking to her breakfast hours hadn't just meant she could spend most afternoons with Rosie. Also, it allowed her to take full advantage of the long summer breaks when GMTV turned itself over to kids' programmes. Over the past few years, she and Rosie had managed to spend six full weeks together each summer. 'I just spent almost every day sitting in the garden watching my baby grow up, which is what life is all about,' she says, hugely grateful that her career choice gave her this wonderful opportunity. Now Rosie was indeed growing up, Lorraine admits that her daughter shares some of her mother's most famous – or possibly infamous – characteristics. 'She's a telly freak and she blathers away all the time,' Lorraine laughs, noting that Rosie somehow manages to sound totally English one minute and very Scottish the next.

The Scottish accent shouldn't have surprised anyone. The

family spent much of their free time commuting up and down over the border and Rosie had built up a small army of friends near her grandparents' house in East Kilbride. Almost all the visits were great fun and problem-free. But in the early summer of 2000 one trip was to end in rare controversy. The local Scots, of all people, would be the ones leading an attack on their most supportive daughter.

It all began when Lorraine and her family took Rosie and some other children out for a play in the park, just as they did during most visits. This time, though, Lorraine wasn't happy. There seemed to be litter, dog dirt, broken glass and graffiti everywhere. This wasn't the East Kilbride she loved and had grown up in – nor was it the East Kilbride she wanted to see ever again. Deciding that things would only get better if enough people stood up and demanded a change, she got ready to be first with her head above the parapet. She spoke to some local journalists about the condition of the play areas, and the girl who had started out reporting on local news suddenly found herself making it. It might have seemed a trivial, local issue, but it soon grabbed headlines across the country.

'When I lived in East Kilbride everything was new and they took pride in keeping everything clean,' she told reporters. 'It is the same old story – 99 per cent of the people take a pride in the local environment and it is just the 1 per cent who ruin things. But you can't be bored in East Kilbride, so there is really no excuse for people to stand around smashing bottles. There is so much for people to do in this town. I'm saying this because I care about the area and because I get home as often as I can. It's a great place to live and a great place for children. I still have a lot of family there and a lot of friends.'

For a while, it seemed as though the local councillors would not be among them. Several prominent dignitaries spoke out to criticise Lorraine in the local and then national press as the silly-season row intensified. Most hinted that as a rich celebrity visitor from down south Lorraine had no right to comment on the surroundings north of the border.

Heading back to Berkshire after the unusually controversial break, Lorraine had to hope that her intervention would produce some positive changes. In the meantime, she was glad she had once more put her beloved East Kilbride on the map. A couple of London-based newspapers had even sent some typically free-spending reporters up to the town to check out the parks for themselves in the slow news days of that early summer period, so she felt she had even managed to pump some extra cash into the local economy, giving her another reason to think that her intervention had been worthwhile. When 'clean our kids' parks' campaigns were launched in and around Glasgow and volunteer forces put together, she was doubly pleased she had risked alienating people by speaking out so publicly.

* * * * *

Lorraine's next visit to Scotland was a sad one – she travelled up for her grandfather's funeral and stayed two days to share the family's mourning. Back in England, as the weather heated up in one of the warmest Junes in years, she found she was feeling unaccountably tired. Few breakfast television presenters say they ever really get used to the early morning alarm calls, especially those whose children stop them having lie-ins at the weekend. But after some fifteen years of pre-dawn starts, Lorraine knew the difference between standard tiredness and the kind of bugs that thrived in stuffy television studios. She ploughed on with her work, desperately hoping she wasn't about to come down with something a good two months before her usual summer break. Like most women, though, she says some instinct must have told her the truth when the tiredness didn't go away. At forty, and six years after Rosie's arrival, she was suddenly convinced that she was pregnant.

She took a test in the early afternoon after returning from a show that had felt far more gruelling than usual and waited to see if her prediction would be confirmed. It was, and while she and Steve were over the moon she was about to start feeling terrible. When she had been carrying Rosie, Lorraine says she felt hugely energised and was hardly sick once. This pregnancy already looked as if it was going to be very different.

'Although it is called morning sickness I actually felt worse in the afternoons. Some mornings, though, on my way into work, I thought I would have to stop the car in order to throw up. But I found that drinking hot ginger tea as soon as I woke up really helped.'

Feeling that at forty she couldn't take any chances, Lorraine cut out booze from the moment she got her test results and took a very close look at her diet. She went on a full-scale listeria-watch, making sure everything she ate was properly cooked and cutting out soft cheeses, runny eggs and all the other foods that are worrying for pregnant woman. At the same time, she tried to get as much rest as possible.

She and Steve decided to keep things a secret in the early days of the pregnancy but organised a trip to Scotland for a quick break. They booked into one of their favourite hideaway hotels for some pampering and relaxation, planning to stop off at Lorraine's parents to tell them the secret news on their return. Both were beaming with excitement as they packed their bags, not least because at the back of their minds was the old wives' tale that said if your second pregnancy is very different to your first, your baby will be the opposite sex. If the rumour was true then Rosie could be looking forward to a baby brother in the spring.

Tragically, this was never to be.

It was when the trio were heading up to the hotel near Oban that Lorraine suddenly felt a series of sharp, stabbing pains in her side. Because no one else knew she was pregnant, she wasn't immediately sure who to call or what to do. Steve suggested her old friend Jacqueline, a nurse and one of their most trusted and sensible friends. After a long chat Lorraine started to feel better – her old excitement about being pregnant had returned and she wanted to continue with their holiday as planned. They checked into their hotel in the tiny hideaway of Port Appin, had a quiet family meal and planned to go for a wander around the coast early the next morning.

At 5am, though, Lorraine woke up feeling terrible and convinced things were going wrong again. She was right. She was bleeding heavily and just after dawn the local doctor confirmed her worst fears. He said it looked as though she had lost her baby, but that she should go straight to hospital for tests and proper care.

With Oban's nearest main hospital some distance away, Lorraine and Steve decided they might as well head all the way home to Ninewells, their own local hospital in Dundee. That way they would be closer to their friends and family in case the news was as bad as the doctor feared.

It was to be a long and terrible journey. Lorraine was feeling worse by the hour, but she was determined to keep it all from Rosie and so she carried on reading her stories and playing their usual car games as Steve steered them across the country towards Dundee. In some ways this enforced jollity helped get everyone through the next two hours. 'I just didn't want Rosie to realise anything was amiss. I had to carry on as if everything was fine. This actually helped me get through because I couldn't get too tearful or panicky as it would have upset my daughter,' Lorraine said afterwards.

By the time they got to hospital she was feeling at her lowest ebb and was preparing to be told the worst. She was having a scan and the nurse was examining and re-examining the images on the screen in front of them. Lorraine was about to get some wonderful news.

'There's something there. There's a heartbeat.'

The nurse looked up from the screen, a huge smile on her face. Lorraine was convinced that she had misheard her and asked for the news again. After being shown the screen herself she could finally believe it. Her baby was still alive. Everything might still be OK.

Doctors say that many women bleed heavily in the early stages of a pregnancy and still go on to have healthy and uncomplicated births. But for this to happen she will need to focus even more carefully on getting plenty of rest. After a long discussion with the doctors, Lorraine and Steve headed home where Lorraine tried to do just that. Both were almost overcome at having been given a second chance. Neither knew that more heartache was just around the corner.

Back at home with Steve looking after Rosie, an exhausted but relieved Lorraine was soon asleep. But after only a couple of hours she was awake, in pain and bleeding again.

Please can this be another false alarm, she prayed. The pains told her otherwise, though. This time she wasn't feeling the sharp, stabbing pains she had suffered on the journey to Oban. This time it was the sort of pain she associated with the first stages of labour. She clung to Steve, trying to believe that all could still be well. But in the end she had lost so much blood that she passed out and a terrified Steve had to call an ambulance. On coming round, her first thoughts, once more, were of Rosie. 'She had slept through most of this and knowing that she might wake up and be frightened actually helped keep me calm.'

When she got to hospital the second time there was to be no good news. After another round of tests it was confirmed that Lorraine had indeed lost her baby, eight weeks into the term.

At home the doubts and regrets began almost immediately. 'Of course you torture yourself afterwards,' Lorraine says of the experience. 'When I had been at my grandfather's funeral, before I knew I was pregnant, I had toasted his life with a couple of enormous whiskies. Could that have had an effect? What about the kind of food I was eating before I knew? I remembered having a Brie sandwich. You aren't supposed to eat soft cheeses. I had had a dental check-up before I knew. Was I pregnant then and would the X-rays have caused problems? On and on, round and round in my head I thought about all these things, because you want to know why it has happened. You think that, if you can find a reason, it might make a bit of sense. And then maybe you could stop it from happening again. But, of course, there often are no reasons.'

Her mum Anne said to reporters that one of the saddest parts of the story was that the first thing most people would ever know about Lorraine's pregnancy was the fact that it was over. 'Lorraine was desperate to say that she was pregnant but wanted to wait a bit longer. She and Steve were really looking forward to telling everyone in a few weeks' time, so they are really upset. Lorraine has been really brave. She'll need some time to get over what has happened.'

Keeping quiet about what had happened wasn't possible because she had been due back on television the day after her Scottish break finished. When she didn't appear her agent and friend Jimmy O'Reilly was forced to explain why. 'She is expected to make a full recovery but of course she is devastated,' he said, at the end of a brief and dignified statement. Cards and letters of sympathy started to arrive at GMTV within hours of the news being reported, some hand delivered, others sent from every corner of the country. Jimmy says they meant a huge amount to his old friend. But for her part Lorraine says one other factor helped her recovery: Rosie. 'Having Rosie meant I couldn't wallow in misery. I couldn't just go to my bed and cry all the time, as much as I wanted to, because I had to think of her. It was the best therapy.'

As her parents headed south to stay with Lorraine in Berkshire, and as friends and other relatives rallied round, Steve once more proved to be worth more than his weight in gold. 'Steve was wonderful throughout and I felt like hugging my friends and family who remembered to ask him how he felt,' Lorraine says. 'So often all the attention and sympathy is given to the women. But husbands and partners suffer, too. They just aren't allowed to show it.'

As usual, work also came to her rescue. Just a week after the news of the miscarriage broke, she was back on screen with *LK Live*. Before the cameras started to roll again, she shared some brief, tearful hugs with friends in the dressing room and on the set. She even shook off the fact that in a piece of awful timing, a mortified guest on the first show back joked about how her football-mad husband had asked her to delay a Caesarean because it clashed with an important game. Afterwards, crew members say it was hard to work out who was the most upset, the show's producers and the guest herself for allowing this kind of subject to be raised on such a sensitive day, or Lorraine for inadvertently making everyone else feel uncomfortable.

Having thrown herself back into work, Lorraine found herself in one of the awkward positions that people in the public eye often face after personal tragedies. She wanted to move on and prove that a miscarriage need not be a defining moment in a woman's life, but every journalist who called her wanted to talk about it, and she was being asked to sit for more interviews and profiles than at any point since joining the main breakfast-TV couch a decade earlier.

She talked to Steve, her parents and close friends about the explosion of interest in her private life. Her agent Jimmy and the publicity staff at GMTV were also consulted. She then decided that giving one big interview on the subject could serve three very important ends. First, she could publicly thank all the people who had written to her sharing their own experiences, often in very detailed and emotional letters. Her second goal was to raise both money and awareness for the charity Tommy's Campaign, which funds research into the causes and prevention of miscarriages. As well as seeing a big donation go to the charity because of the interview, Lorraine made it a condition of the article being published that information on The Miscarriage Association be given at the end of the interview. That way she felt readers could get the support and advice that would see them through the crisis.

Finally, Lorraine was hoping that by speaking out once then she could, indeed, move on from this issue – 'If I keep talking about it, people will say it is all I ever think about and that's not the case.' Life, she said, had to go on.

With GMTV at last on its summer break and Lorraine happily spending all day with Rosie, she felt she had achieved all three of her goals. Her life was never to be quite the same again, however. These experiences would always be at the back of her mind when similar subjects came up on her programme again, or in day-to-day conversations. From now on, the woman famous for talking at a hundred miles an hour would always try to slow down to make sure nothing she said could inadvertently hurt the feelings of any women who had suffered a similar crisis. And when her old pal and colleague Fiona Phillips also suffered a miscarriage less than six months later, Lorraine was one of the first to comfort her.

* * * * *

Ironically enough, children would be the focus of Lorraine's life throughout the autumn of 2000. Friends and family had always said they loved the long stories she made up for Rosie, and an educational publisher reckoned they could be bestsellers. So after talking to plenty of teachers and social workers about the gaps in many young kids' imaginations, she put together the Fun-To-Learn series of books. They were aimed at children aged between six months and four years and Lorraine's hope was that she could pass on some of the tips she had picked up as a working mother. 'They are an extension of the stories I have told Rosie and I've tried to make sure they are educational without being po-faced,' she said of the four board books and two storybooks. 'Once you start teaching children, they are like sponges who just want to learn more and more. But it should be fun and not a chore. Children soak up so much. Good parents need to build on this all the time.'

Maybe a decade down the line, perhaps when she gives up most of her television work, Lorraine says she dreams of writing adult fiction – something in the style of Maeve Binchy – possibly basing a book on the life of her grandmother, Margaret McMahon. 'She was an ordinary Scotswoman who was very bright and should have gone to university but instead had to work. She had sixteen children, only eight of whom survived. There may be nothing out of this world about her life, but I think people would be interested in reading about someone like her,' Lorraine muses.

If this ever gets off the ground then she certainly has a good publishing track record to use as a calling card. Long before Jamie Oliver got on the case, Lorraine was part of an Eating For Life campaign aimed at improving the food kids eat at school, for example. Then she joined forces with nutritionist Anita Bean to produce *Lorraine Kelly's Baby & Toddler Eating Plan* – with one very serious intention. 'Making sure your children eat well and healthily is a big responsibility and you need to send out all the right messages. If you are always on a faddy diet or sit glowering at a lettuce leaf, then your children will pick up on that, even at a very early age.' Once again, she brought in her own experiences, making the book as down to earth as it could be. There would be no ridiculous demands for meals to be made with organic pomegranates or Persian saffron. In Lorraine's world, no recipe would need more than an hour to prepare and cook. She reckons she knows full well how little time most mums have to work on food and how desperate they are not to feel a prisoner in their kitchens. 'But I'm still convinced you can give your child good, healthy meals,' she said.

As if to prove it, the amount of time Lorraine was to have to prepare any of Rosie's meals was to face a cut from September because her flagship morning show was being given a longer, one-hour slot. The upgrade was evidence of just how popular she had become. The original *Nine O'Clock Live* slot, given to her as a way of easing her back into work after Rosie's birth, had turned into a central part of the breakfast schedule under all its new names. Her ratings frequently topped the five million mark, and with so many advertisers prepared to pay premium prices to have their products seen in her commercial breaks it was an obvious decision to offer her more air time.

Filling the extended slot was tricky, however. Viewers would feel short-changed if all Lorraine did was to double the length of her existing items or pad things out with unnecessarily long interviews. So she spent a lot of the summer in meetings with the producers trying to come up with a new running order that would give everyone value for money.

Her own finances, however, were the least important part of the deal. Many other presenters, on being told they were to double their hours, would fight for a golden new pay rate and claim persecution if they were denied it. Lorraine was different. The fighter from the Gorbals was well aware of television's going rate and of how much she was worth to all the major broadcasters. But she was equally aware of how little many of her friends in other jobs were paid, and how much harder many of her studio guests worked just to make ends meet. Lorraine Kelly would never forget her roots – and when the subject of money comes up she hardly draws breath as she gives her views.

'Anyone who works in this industry is bloody lucky and should be grateful! I think I get paid far too much. Although I don't get paid nearly as much as people say I do, it's still very good money for what we do. It's not an easy job but it's not like being a brain surgeon. It's not standing on your feet all day working in a shop or waitressing, both of which I've done. And that's the trouble with some people in television – they can take it a bit too seriously.'

But isn't presenting a live television show in front of millions of viewers every day a stressful thing to do? she was asked. Her reply was equally forthright. 'Being stressed is having no money and three children to feed. What I do is nowhere near as stressful as that. I take my work seriously because I appreciate how lucky I am. There aren't that many people who get up at half past five in the morning who are going to have a nice day. There are shift workers doing really tough jobs for the National Health Service, getting thruppence ha'penny. I get up early but I finish early. Not many working mothers can pick their kid up from school, but I can. I love what I do and I shouldn't say it because my bosses might read it, but I would do it for a lot less,' she said of the pay rise she earned for turning *LK Today* into an hour-long show.

The longer show did, of course, raise Lorraine's profile once more. But she tried to deflect as much of the attention as possible. 'I've never wanted to be in the headlines and I suppose I have done it all rather quietly,' she says of her move up the career ladder. 'Some people court hype but I don't. If I started coming on like some prima donna my husband and family would squish me. Years ago, when Anne Diamond left

TV-am and I eventually took over from her, nobody blew a trumpet and said I was the new Anne Diamond. I would have hated that. I could have gone out and hired a press agent but I was too busy getting on with the job.'

This ability to get on with the job was one of the many things that Lorraine's producers loved about her, and one of the many reasons why she had survived so long in such a competitive and famously back-stabbing industry. A genuine sense of modesty was another factor, as *Sunday Times* reporter Lynn Cochrane discovered when she spoke to Lorraine just after Judy Finnegan defected to Channel 4 with Richard Madeley. 'I said that with Judy gone, Lorraine can rightfully claim her title as Queen of Daytime TV,' says Lynn.

'Oh shut up, shut up, shut up!' was Lorraine's initial reply. Quickly followed by: 'Oh Christ no! No, no, no, no, no, no!'

The extra elements in the hour-long show helped give her a new enthusiasm for what she did. As ever, she was dismissed as being lightweight. But just as before there was more depth to what she did than many people realised. And Lorraine thrived on the contrasts. 'I'm so lucky that I get up in the morning and I actually want to go into the studio. Not many people can say that about the jobs that they do. I have always said that if I got up in the morning and didn't want to do my job that would be the time to call it a day. But how could you possibly do that when every single day is different? I might start off the day discussing shoes or lipstick or whatever, but then you might be talking to someone who has been a hostage in the Middle East, or maybe Gordon Brown or Tony Blair.' No one, the critics say with a smile, can go from mascara to massacres with the smoothness of Lorraine Kelly.

The extra beauty of her show is the simple fact that she is

able to be herself throughout. If she likes something or somebody she will say so. And if she disapproves, she won't hide it. Television critics say this honesty is one of the key foundations on which her bond with her fans is built. As well as the fact that most of the time she isn't just saying what she thinks – she's saying what *we* think as well –'I'd find it hard to adopt a personality that was alien. Being able to be myself is a real privilege.'

Unfortunately for fans, Lorraine's fundamental good nature means she won't do the one thing many of us might secretly hope she will – dishing the dirt on her co-hosts or famous guests. Dirt was certainly in demand in the boom days of GMTV when sparks flew between Eamonn Holmes and Anthea Turner. While she knows more than most about what was really going on between the pair, Lorraine has vowed to say nothing, saying it would be wrong of her to pass it on. 'I certainly don't believe in getting involved in public slanging matches with my fellow presenters. What happened between Eamonn and Anthea was awful. It was very silly and I am glad it is all behind us,' she said, when the dust had settled and Anthea had left for pastures new. 'Separately they are lovely people, but I wouldn't have them to dinner on the same night,' was as close as she would go to admitting how bad things had become off camera.

As well as being discrete, Lorraine soon proved she could also be a fiercely protective friend, should the need arise. One occasion when it did was in 2000, when Anthea Turner was suddenly transformed into the most hated woman in the land following the debacle of the so-called 'Flakegate' scandal at her wedding. *OK!* magazine, who sponsored the wedding, released to the media a photo of Anthea and her new husband,

Grant Bovey, enjoying the latest Cadbury's Snowflake bars. It was published in the *Sun* with the headline 'Sickener', and the couple were accused of using their celebrity wedding to promote the chocolate, which they strongly denied. Desperate to take the heat off her old pal and realising that a bit of humour might help diffuse the situation, Lorraine was ready with a joke at her own expense. 'I want to take issue with the tabloids who said I was spotted eating the Snowflake bar at Anthea's wedding. I didn't eat one of them – I ate eight of them,' she told Carol Malone of the *Sunday Mirror*.

When it comes to her favourite guests she is prepared to talk, however, and some of her thoughts are a surprise. The broadcaster and writer Clive James gets top marks for being one of the wittiest, most interesting, most intellectual and least patronising men Lorraine has ever met. She first interviewed him back in her early days on TV-am when she first moved to London and says it is still one of her most treasured memories. Hollywood legend Kirk Douglas is another man Lorraine interviewed very early on in her career and one she has never forgotten. She says she was incredibly nervous when she met the star – not least because she knew Kirk's biggest fan (Lorraine's mother) would be glued to her television set at home. 'In the end I needn't have worried because he was such a charmer, a real true star who just worked his magic and left us with a real glow.'

Joan Collins is another favourite – again of both Lorraine and her mum. 'She is fabulous, a very sharp and clever lady,' says Lorraine. 'My mum had given me a copy of a book she wanted Joan to sign, which she did straightaway. She's a professional and she always remembers to thank everybody when she leaves.' Kate Winslet was someone else Lorraine bonded with when they met for an interview – saying the actress was a true professional even though she was going through a difficult time in her personal life.

Victoria Beckham gets a rare thumbs-up from Lorraine as well – the two hit it off when they headed out for what was supposed to be a glitzy on-camera shopping trip and ended up having a far from glamorous conversation about being a mum and walking around the house all day in tracksuit bottoms with baby sick down your back! Lorraine also raves about the singer k. d. Lang. 'She is my heroine and I will never forget the day she was on my show, standing next to me and singing live. I nearly lost it. I had to think about Maggie Thatcher naked to stop myself from crying,' Lorraine says with typical humour.

Belying her lightweight reputation, she also says two of her personal career highlights are the interviews she did with writers Norman Mailer and Gore Vidal. The bookworm in her meant she had already read most of their works before speaking to them. But she poured over them all one more time before the big day, in order to get the most out of this rare chance to pick their brains and find out what makes them tick. She says she peppered both men with questions before and after the actual interviews, and while she admits that neither had expected much from a breakfast television presenter, she hopes they left the studio feeling she at least knew her stuff.

Staying on top of things means that Lorraine throws off her 'mumsy' image and embraces almost every piece of new technology she finds. She had a mobile phone when they were the size of bricks, carried a laptop around when it weighed more than a suitcase and now jokes that she gets cold sweats at the thought of losing her Blackberry. Away from the GMTV offices, she continues to put in the hours on her other projects and after putting Rosie to bed, she is frequently at her computer after 10pm researching for future shows, writing occasional magazine articles or putting together promotions for her favoured charities. She denies, however, that she is superwoman. 'It only works because I've got a brilliant husband who does more than his fair share,' she admits. 'He cooks, he goes to the supermarket. Now, that's pretty good. I don't believe in superwoman and women having it all and all that nonsense. I don't think you can. So if I'm working late, Steve will make the tea and so on, which is what makes it all work.'

The rest of her family and friends also help out whenever possible. Lorraine's dad always volunteers to wash her car and do DIY when he and Anne come down to stay in Berkshire, while best friend Joyce is one of Rosie's favourite babysitters. Lorraine has also grown increasingly close to her brother over the years, even though Graham now lives far away in Singapore, where he fell in love with a local girl, Saleemah ('She speaks English with a great Scottish accent,' big sis Lorraine is proud to say). Visiting the couple in their new home was one of the biggest trips Rosie had ever taken, and as well as enjoying being fussed over by the stewardesses on the flight, she loved the heat and the noise of their ultimate destination, Lorraine reports.

Back in Britain, the competitive streak that lies deep within Lorraine's mind will often rear its head when she speaks to Graham and they talk about their joint love of travel. But his sister, for once, feels at a disadvantage. 'I'll phone him up on his mobile and say: Where are you? And he'll say: Vietnam, or somewhere wonderful. And he'll say: Where are you? And I'll say: Nowhere. Slough.' The boy who spent years being put down and pinched by his mouthy big sister could finally get the last word.

14

THE NATION'S FAVOURITE

*'This year's top hairstyle is called the shag and today
our resident stylist is here to give our model one.'*

'**W**hat do you look like first thing in the morning?'
It is the standard question for anyone on breakfast
television and Lorraine always has a two-word answer: 'Not
wonderful.'

She tends to be the first to wake in the Kelly household and
says she tiptoes around the bedroom 'like a wee *Tom & Jerry*
cartoon' to avoid waking Steve. It's not as much fun as it
sounds. 'I've been getting up early now since 1988 but I don't
think your body ever really gets used to it. I'm lucky that I can
manage on five hours' sleep but it's tough and I don't necessarily
like it,' she says. Her GMTV car is normally outside the house
from around 6am and by the time Steve goes on breakfast and
school run duty for Rosie, Lorraine has read half the papers,
had a quick doze and made it as far as west London.

On the days when she fills in for other presenters' holidays
or sicknesses on the main GMTV sofa, her mornings start
even earlier. Yet she takes it all in her stride – as *Sunday Times*

reporter Lynn Cochrane found when she too got up long before dawn to watch the lady in action. 'I slump, bleary-eyed, watching Lorraine Kelly on daytime television and the pace would floor Red Rum,' was how she described the experience. 'She has already introduced an Irish band, Bellefire – "beautiful, beautiful girls" – finished a piece on two elderly members of a deaf/blind charity who found love – "Peter, what a man, a true romantic" – while all the time continually urging the nation to "get up and give" for the programme's annual fundraiser. It is still not yet 7.30am.'

Two hours later, when the main show and her own show were finished, Lorraine was still on top form and looking fresh as a daisy, says Lynn. She then sprang a surprise, reaching into her bag for a handful of old snapshots she had brought in to give to Lynn's photographer. 'One of the pictures showed her wearing a tartan suit, bright red lipstick, and huge, dangly earrings,' Lynn remembers. 'It was taken on her first day at GMTV and she looks like something off the lid of a shortbread tin. But it says something about Lorraine, however, that in this age when even D-list celebrities demand airbrushing and photo and copy approval for articles, she has raided her home album to provide us with such a cheesy snap.'

Other reporters sent to meet Lorraine to write profiles tell similar stories about how easy-going she can be. 'I'll just go for a wee, then I'll be right with you,' is how one feature writer told of the unconventional opening gambit she had for him when they met behind the scenes at the GMTV studios. Often, the other big surprise for Lorraine's interviewers is what she is wearing. Comfort, rather than fashion, is her number one priority. 'If I didn't do the job I do, I would only possess one posh frock and loads of comfy clothes. If I was just on radio, I don't think I would even own a skirt,' she muses. This anti-celebrity state of mind was yet another factor that endeared Lorraine to her fans. But was her down-to-earth nature about to trigger a career crisis?

The question was asked in September 2000. Lorraine and Steve settled down at home for another quiet night in front of the television. Both are big fans of topical comedy shows so the latest series of BBC 1's *Alistair McGowan's Big Impression* was an obvious choice to watch. Tonight they were going to get a big shock, however.

After winning huge praise for her brilliant take-offs of everyone from Posh Spice to Barbara Windsor, Alistair's hugely talented sidekick Ronni Ancona was about to unveil some new spoof sketches. One of them was of Lorraine – and when they saw it Lorraine and Steve were almost crying with laughter. Ronni's incarnation saw Lorraine as extraordinarily and unremittingly jolly – the 100 per cent mumsy and lightweight cliché that has dogged her since her first day on the main TV-am sofa. 'It was very, very funny and uncannily like me,' Lorraine said, through gritted teeth. It also reminded her of just how often she used the key words 'great' and 'brilliant' to the exclusion of all others.

Lorraine's management team and the GMTV staff had long since got used to seeing their star presenter compared to a manic version of Mrs Doubtfire. But as everyone digested the *Big Impression* show, there were serious worries that this latest spoof might be taking the joke a step too far.

Everyone in the entertainment industry is aware that being parodied can do wonders for some people's careers. Being talked about, after all, is better than being ignored. And celebrities can win new fans if they are good enough sports to play along with the jokes. But everyone is concerned about the so-called tipping point when the comedy version of a star can become so ingrained in the national consciousness that it causes huge damage to the reality. The key example of this came when Harrie Enfield's spoof DJs Smashie and Nicie started sending up the awfulness of many mainstream radio presenters. It was all meant to be taken in good humour, but the powers that be at Radio One seemed to feel that the comedy characters rang a little bit too true. In particular, the Radio One line-up never survived the parody – the likes of Simon Bates, Dave Lee Travis, Gary Davies and more all left the station soon afterwards to be replaced by a younger, supposedly more credible crew. Could Lorraine's career be mortally hit by a similar spoof?

Fortunately, it seemed that her fan base was too deep for even the most nervous studio executive to risk axing her. And with a big smile, she headed to the studio determined to severely ration her use of the words 'great' and 'brilliant'. 'Make sure you tell me if I start repeating them too often again,' she told the studio staff, after making everyone roar with laughter by running through a mock interview of herself, playing Ronni Ancona, playing herself.

But if she thought becoming a figure of fun in the comedy world was her final embarrassment of the season she was wrong. She (and, more specifically, her infamously Scottish accent) was about to get a public dressing down on live television that would have done a *Big Impression* sketch proud. It happened when actress Greta Scacchi joined her on the sofa to promote her role in a West End play. The pair seemed to be chatting easily about the role, the state of London's theatreland, Hollywood and all the other issues of the moment, and Lorraine was convinced all was going well. She was wrong.

'Can I say one thing?' Greta asked, suddenly.

'Of course you can,' Lorraine replied.

'I know that you have got a funny accent and pronounce lots of words strangely but my name is Scacchi. I wouldn't want you to perpetuate the mispronunciation. Most people call me Scatchie, but it is Scacchi.'

Mortified at the public rebuke (and secretly convinced that she hadn't made a mistake when she had first introduced the actress), Lorraine brushed the comment aside with aplomb. 'It is emblazoned. I will never get it wrong again,' she told her guest, tongue imperceptibly in cheek. Afterwards, Lorraine got the last word, as she usually does. 'She apologised and told me she was trying to be funny. Obviously comedy isn't her strong point,' Lorraine said of the spat.

By coincidence, she herself was making several inroads into the world of comedy at this time. First up came a walk-on part in the final series of her favourite British sitcom, *One Foot In The Grave*. She was asked to appear alongside fellow Scots Richard Wilson and Annette Crosby in the show's fifth and final series.

Fortunately for someone who admits she had never even appeared in any school plays when she was younger, Lorraine's role didn't require a great deal of theatrical training – she was playing a breakfast television star who interviews a TV doctor played by the show's writer David Renwick. Their topic was irritable bowel syndrome and Richard Wilson's Victor Meldrew manages to convince himself that he is a sufferer – with typically ridiculous results. 'It was such a great day,' said Lorraine of her sitcom debut (they filmed it in just two takes) and she then persuaded Richard and Annette to come on to GMTV as her special guests to talk it over a little more.

Next, and also because she felt like having a laugh and cheering herself up after a rough year, Lorraine agreed to be interviewed on *The Frank Skinner Show* to help write and present a documentary on Sheena Easton called *Never Can Say Goodbye* and then to appear as a panellist on *Never Mind the Buzzcocks*. Showbusiness experts say the latter was a particularly clever choice. 'One of the problems Lorraine has always had as a performer is that many of the people with strong opinions about her have never actually seen her shows,' says agent Leon Kinleigh. 'They have an idea in their heads that she is fluffy, lightweight and faintly ridiculous because they think all breakfast television stars are like that. As long as she made a success of it, then going on a young adult show like *Buzzcocks* was a great way to dispel some of these opinions and win her some new credibility.'

As it turned out, Lorraine scored a minor hit on *Buzzcocks* – but she says she had no cynical plan to win new fans in the process. It just happened to be one of the shows she and Steve most enjoyed watching – and both were big fans of its host Mark Lamarr. Having felt surprisingly comfortable in the world of panel-based comedy shows, she decided to see the year out with another one when she said yes to a long-standing invitation to be a guest on *Have I Got News For You* alongside Paul Merton and Ian Hislop. Angus Deayton was in the host's chair and Lorraine's fellow guest was Liberal Democrat MP Lembit Opik.

Regular viewers of the show can attest that many first-time panellists suffer badly on the programme. Some try – and fail

– to use it as a showcase for their own supposed humour. Others seem simply too overawed to even speak. Lorraine, though, was deemed a surprise hit as a guest, not least because she was clearly better informed about current events than many had expected. 'Fortunately I've always been a bit of a news junkie and can watch CNN and Sky News for hours,' she said, when asked how she had prepared to face the potential wrath of Merton and Hislop. 'The key is to not try and be a smart ass with the others because they are just so sharp and can annihilate anyone. But with me, the guys were all friendly and helped me relax,' she said of her début.

'Kelly proved herself an extremely sharp tool in the box, pre-empting the thoughts of both Deayton and Merton, and having a whale of a time in the process,' said one media commentator of her first show. A typical exchange proves the point.

'Americans seem to have a problem using the word "pregnant" when describing un-punched voting chads,' said Angus of the Florida voting scandal that was dominating the headlines that autumn.

'But they are happy to advertise pile cream and all that on television,' added Lorraine.

'Not quite the same,' commented Angus.

'Oh no, the two go together, believe you me,' rejoined Lorraine, as the women in the audience led a huge burst of applause.

At the post-show drinks party in the stuffy 'green room' close to the top of the London Studios building, Lorraine said she could never understand why other people didn't share her passion for politics. 'Am I political? Oh yes! I think everybody must be. You must be. How can you not be?' she asks.

When a reporter once asked her if she was going to vote in the next General Election she went ballistic at the thought that she wouldn't. 'Women chained themselves to railings and were force fed to get the right to vote. So you've got to vote, you've absolutely got to.'

She is also surprisingly well connected – not least because over the years she has met a huge number of politicians, including Gordon Brown, while travelling on the so-called 'tartan shuttle' flights from London to Scotland on Friday and Sunday nights. Her actual political allegiance isn't hard to determine. 'I've got a really simplistic view, I suppose. It probably seems as I am the most naïve person in the world but I just really believe that if you've got it then you should give to people who haven't.'

She says the gap between rich and poor is perhaps the one thing she would take to the streets to protest about – though she supports a host of other social causes in less public ways and has no intention of stopping. When plans were announced to axe or merge six of Scotland's historic infantry regiments, for example, she sent a personal message of support to the campaign to save them. It put her alongside the likes of SNP leader Alex Salmon and soon-to-be Liberal Democrat leader Menzies Campbell. Neither man seemed at all surprised to have Lorraine in their company – not least because both knew her well from the Tartan Shuttle.

Interestingly enough, Lorraine's in-built social conscience also dovetails with her life-long obsession with diets – and with her growing belief that they are both destructive and ineffective. 'I can't stand the way that women tell themselves they've been good because they've not eaten today. I just think: Why exactly do you think you were good? Did you help a wee old lady across the road, or did you give £100 to charity? No, you never ate a cake all day and you think you deserve a round of applause. It's mad.'

* * * * *

'If you could just sign here.'

It was the spring of 2001 and Lorraine Kelly was about to put her name to a unique, lucrative but ultimately ill-fated deal with Sky Television. She was hugely enjoying having an extra half hour for her main GMTV show, and her bosses wanted to extend her hours even more. They reckoned their star presenter could easily fill an hour and a half every day – but the problem was that the television regulators wouldn't let her. Under the terms of its licence, GMTV had to pull the plug and hand over to ITV at 9.30 every morning. Everyone felt it was a ridiculous situation (especially as Lorraine's ratings at that point in the morning were at near record levels) but no one knew what to do about it, until Sky came along.

The upstart broadcaster was about to launch a new assault on the daytime market by beefing up its Sky One line-up. Its bosses were convinced that Lorraine and her team were the ideal people to help them so Sky offered GMTV a deal. They could produce a whole new show for Lorraine after the 9.30am cut-off and it would be broadcast on Sky via a host of new digital and satellite feeds. 'Basically, at 9.20 I say goodbye to GMTV, someone will do something fabulous with a switch and a few minutes later I will be on Sky, in the same clothes,' she said of the new deal, failing to explain that she also had just four minutes to get from the old GMTV studio to the sparkling new Sky set next door. 'It's a bit like having a new job but you know where the toilets and the canteen are.'

For the broadcasting industry as a whole it was a bit more than this, though. 'The deal was the first sign of a war between the major broadcasters over the daytime schedule where things are about to get very heated,' said media analyst Paul Johnson. 'With Richard and Judy off to Channel 4 and ITV still unsure of who will replace them, Sky knows it has a superb chance to catch up with the big boys. These are going to be very exciting times for the breakfast and daytime market.'

As she signed the deal, Lorraine knew that for all her jokes about the flicking of switches it was going to mean a lot of work. The first show wouldn't be broadcast until September, when all the new breakfast and daytime schedules came back after the summer break. But in the meantime she and the producers would spend a lot of time working on a new look, feel and running order for the show. The only thing that didn't take long to arrange was its title. Lorraine was the big name that Sky wanted, so *Lorraine* was to be the one-word title for the new show.

After the contract was signed, she and Steve talked for hours about the new challenge. As usual, a big part of their discussion focused on the effect the new job might have on Rosie, but as she would be in school when Lorraine was on air this didn't seem to be a problem. Even after the daily post-mortem on the show, Lorraine knew she would be home in time to pick her daughter up from school. Something else was bothering her, though.

Ever since she had left her reporting role and become studio-based Lorraine had taken to wearing contact lenses on air. No one had ever told her to do so, but she says she was aware of an 'unwritten rule' saying key presenters couldn't wear glasses – even if they were a former Spectacle Wearer of the Year. The problem was that Lorraine's eyes were finding her lenses harder and harder to take. She dramatically cut back on the time she wore them, putting them in at exactly 8.22am, just before *LK Today*, and whipping them back out as soon as she had said her on-screen goodbyes. 'When we got the go ahead for *Lorraine* on Sky, I realised I would have to keep my lenses in for the whole morning, so I decided to do something about it.' That something was laser treatment, which she researched with typical thoroughness before going ahead. After deciding it was safe, she headed to a London hospital for the operation. Less than two hours later she was on her way home, saying the £2,000 bill was the only painful thing about the process. 'As soon as I got home I sat down with a chocolate orange and a glass of champagne and watched *Coronation Street*. Amazingly, I could see it without my specs, which was wonderful.'

Back at work her colleagues joked that with a bit of luck Lorraine might also have more luck with her scripts now that she had 20/20 vision. She tended to be so confident in front of the cameras that she frequently ad-libbed her way past the words on the autocues – and not always with the best results. 'This year's top hairstyle is called the shag and today our resident stylist is here to give our model one,' she told GMTV viewers that spring, as the crew in the studio and galley all collapsed with laughter.

As news of the new Sky show broke, few people doubted her ability to cope with the challenge. Taking on more work had never been a problem for her, nor would it now. 'Lorraine talks quickly, walks quickly, does everything quickly,' said media commentator Simon Hattenstone after meeting her on the GMTV set that spring. She could hardly disagree.

'I don't fanny about, I'm not one of life's fanny abouters – I just get on and do it. I tend to be doing three or four different things at one time,' she told him, admitting that she didn't slow down out of the studio either. When she takes Rosie swimming and her daughter wants a few seconds longer than her mum thinks is strictly necessary for drying her hair, Lorraine says she struggles to hold back. 'She'll stand there, doing her hair, going dadadadah and I'm, like, let's go, let's go! I'm a terrible let's go person. I hate being late and I always try to be at every appointment bang on time.'

She also seemed to have perfected the art of talking without the need to draw breath, Simon decided, saying her words 'cascaded out, faster and faster,' as she warmed to her theme. But punctuality was important to her because she knew a lot of people relied on her following up on all her commitments.

That spring, for example, she signed up to be a team captain in a new quiz show, *A Question of TV*, which was designed as a companion piece to the long-running *A Question of Sport*. 'I'm the female Ally McCoist,' laughed Lorraine as she prepared to film the pilot show. Roland Rivron was the other team captain with Gaby Roslin as the Sue Barker-style referee. A twelve-strong team of producers, writers and crew were working on the project with them, all desperately hoping that it succeeded. In the notoriously insecure world of television a hit show can pay the bills for some time while a flop can be a disaster. For everyone's sake Lorraine wanted to pull out all the stops to generate a hit. Fortunately, the laughs were genuine from the very start. 'It's the best fun I've had doing anything in ages,' she said of the pilot episodes. 'Rowland is the funniest man I have ever met and I was constantly laughing my head off. There were a couple of times when I was laughing so much that I couldn't speak.' And it's not often Lorraine is lost for words.

With the pilot episode being shown to potential broadcasters and a filming schedule being drawn up for a full first series, Lorraine got ready for her next challenge. Smiling broadly and loving every minute, she slipped into a New York Police Department uniform, complete with handcuffs and baton, for a photo shoot to promote a four-day stint for *LK Today* in the Big Apple. 'Sadly, I don't think I will be appearing on the show itself in the uniform because I don't think you are allowed to and I might get into trouble. But it's a really nice uniform and you end up swaggering when you walk,' she said, correctly predicting that the images would soon be joining all the others on the growing number of websites set up in her honour.

The flying visit to America was bad for the body clock but proved good for ratings. Lorraine's plan was to showcase all the beauty, lifestyle, fitness and entertainment trends in the city, and as it was far warmer in May than it had been on her last visit for Joyce's fortieth birthday she didn't feel the need to wrap up like an Eskimo between shows. Having travelled to the city for work or pleasure nearly a dozen times, Lorraine felt she had a good understanding of what made it tick – though she didn't entirely feel at home there. 'Quentin Crisp said New York was like bathing in champagne and it's true it has a zing, you feel like you are in a movie. I just love getting off the plane and jumping into a yellow taxi. It's a fantastic place to visit but I wouldn't want to live here. Manhattan women are very scary. They are all like the girls in *Sex In The City*. You see all these predatory women running around in trainers with sexy slingbacks in their bags and heels that would take the eye out of a fly.'

For one of the final GMTV shows from America Lorraine and the team got into their yellow taxis and were taken over to the Twin Towers in the financial district. They whizzed up the elevators to the 106th floor of the North Tower and broadcast the show live from the iconic Windows On The World restaurant. All of Manhattan lay out behind them and the crew says the staff in the Tower were kind and generous hosts.

Within months, of course, the restaurant, the Towers and probably many of those same waiters and waitresses were gone. September 11, 2001 was a day few people can ever forget. The following morning, Lorraine was on air from London as the aftermath of the tragedy and all its wider implications began to filter through. While the news and political teams were there to cover the details of the story, she had another role to play.

'I am allowed to be myself on GMTV, I don't need to act. So on GMTV the morning after the tragedy I felt scared, and I said so. There's nothing wrong with wondering what the hell was happening and what could happen. I thought of my daughter Rosie and I worried, but I'm allowed to. I thought also of how in New York it had been just a normal day for normal people doing their jobs. I said that as well. I said what I thought, what I was feeling because I think it is important to be able to express yourself honestly when these things happen.'

On a happier note, she had spent some of her time that summer preparing to act as big sister to *Big Brother* contestant Helen Adams – the Welsh hairdresser who infamously liked blinking and was being lined up to appear on *Lorraine* as a beauty expert. Over on GMTV, Lorraine was more worried about stopping one of her colleagues from leaving than about preparing for any new arrivals. There had been persistent rumours that Eamonn Holmes was finally going to give up his place on the main GMTV sofa, and there were growing rumours that Lorraine would start her day a lot earlier by replacing him. 'Go back to getting up at 3am every morning? No thanks!' was her far from subtle response to the story. 'I won't let Eamon go, I'll nail him to the sofa to keep him here if I have to.'

Her forthright side was also given an extra outing that summer when she was asked to appear on *Room 101* with Paul Merton. Famous name guests are asked to provide a list of all the things or people they would like consigned to oblivion in the 101 bin. But would someone as nice as Lorraine be able to come up with the goods? The producers need not have worried. 'Paul said I gave them the longest list of anyone who has ever been on the show,' she admitted, horrified. The model, actress and hopeful Hollywood mogul Liz Hurley was at the top of it. Earlier in the year, Hurley had made the front pages by wearing a typically revealing outfit while a guest at a friend's wedding. Lorraine was quick to speak out. 'The first rule of sisterhood is don't upstage the bride. That was wrong, very wrong,' she said of La Hurley's attention-seeking outfit.

But that wasn't all. 'I don't like anything about her,' Lorraine revealed to Paul when the show was recorded. 'Her accent is very odd too. Even the Queen doesn't speak like that.' There was more. 'She has built herself up as a Hollywood player then crossed a picket line,' Lorraine said of the recent débâcle involving a controversial strike in America. 'I knew of the actors' strike, even my mum knew, so how could someone who pretends to be in the business not know?' If it was any compensation to Liz, she was far from alone in Lorraine's bad books. Her initial list was scaled back to suit the programme's length and Liz was joined in the sin bin with the likes of Bobbie Charlton's hairstyle, Furbies and thongs.

Meanwhile, back at GMTV, her next challenge was to prepare for the annual *Get Up and Give* fund-raising events on the TV station. For reasons that escaped her the moment she said 'yes', Lorraine had agreed that if viewers offered enough cash she would hoof it on stage as Anna in a one-off excerpt from *The King And I*. The musical was winning rave reviews in London's West End, having just opened with Elaine Paige as its leading lady.

Lorraine was not exactly sure she had what it took to follow in Elaine's footsteps, however. 'I knew I was in trouble when I went on stage for the first rehearsal and the musical director said: "Miss Kelly, which key do you sing in?" Oh dear, oh dear, oh dear! The only other time I have sung on television was on the Frank Skinner show when I pretended to be a Proclaimer. All that was required there was to shout in a Scottish accent, and not surprisingly that is something I am able to do. Otherwise, all I do is sing show tunes in the bath sometimes, and I'm pretty bad at that.'

At first, everyone was sure it was just false modesty on her part. 'She told me she has two left feet and can't sing, dance or act,' the *Guardian*'s Simon Hattenstone said as she prepared for her début. 'Oh come on, you're just being modest, give us a twirl!' he said. 'Eventually she did, and she was as good as her word,' he concluded, as Lorraine's left feet made their presence felt.

After some intensive voice and movement training she did get the hang of the act and on a closed set she took to the stage with the Hawaiian actor Keo Woolford, who was playing the King in the West End. The pair recorded a performance of the long 'Shall We Dance' number, and while most people were impressed, Lorraine remained typically self-deprecating. 'Viewers will have to dig deep before I go public with this,' she told the producers after looking at the tapes in the GMTV editing suite. But they were prepared to do just that, and Lorraine's one and only stage role was one of the highlights of the 2001 *Get Up And Give* campaign.

As well as raising plenty of cash, the routine proved just how valuable Lorraine was to GMTV, and how even her mistakes won fans. Who else, for example, could have got away with this, shortly after her 'Shall We Dance' 'moment'. 'Later, we will be looking at some very intimate pictures of the Queen that used to belong to the Royal Family's gynaecologist – oops, I think I must mean genealogist!' she said, while her producers sat aghast in the galley.

Away from the studio, she was also having fun in 2001. She and Graham Norton got together for a wild day out co-presenting the gay Mardi Gras festival in London – reinforcing Lorraine's position as one of the least likely gay icons in the country.

* * * * *

In private, Lorraine and Steve tried not to get upset as the first anniversary of her miscarriage passed. But Lorraine knew the years were going by very quickly. She still wondered if there might be a chance to extend their family. 'I never wanted a big family but I would definitely like more children. But I'm forty one and it's getting more difficult,' she said that autumn. 'I cheered when I saw the picture of Denise Welch and her baby because whenever I hear of a woman in her forties having children I'm thinking: There's still hope!' When Cherie Blair revealed she was pregnant again at forty five Lorraine got the biggest boost of all.

She knew everything had to be kept in perspective and was always worried about the effect her words could have on others, though. 'I don't like to use the word "trying" for another child because it makes us sound like we're at it all the time. But me and Steve are still working on it and having fun doing so. If it happens then it happens,' was how she chose to close the subject for the time being.

* * * * *

With the switch being flicked every morning so that *Lorraine* could go on air for Sky at 9.30am, its host could be excused for turning down any other offers. Her agent was constantly being sent proposals for new daytime and evening shows but none of them seemed right, until one came along which combined three of her key interests: the public at large, raising money for good causes and Scotland. The show, *Town to Town*, was an all-Scottish production in which teams of fifty locals from two towns competed against each other to try and raise the most money for charity. It could have been chaotic, stressful stuff, but Lorraine's easy banter with the huge groups of sometimes punchy, sometimes nervous contestants made it come together in time for the edit. Audiences were never quite as convinced, though, and the programme never made it south of the border or into a second series.

Had she wanted to, Lorraine could have followed up *Town to Town* with something with a far higher profile. She was one of the first big names to be approached by the representatives of production company Granada. They had what seemed like a crazy idea. A diverse group of celebrities were to be put in a makeshift camp somewhere deep in the Australian jungle. The presenters Ant and Dec would watch and commentate on what went on in the camp, and the celebrities would have to pass various challenges in order to win extra rations. Oh, and there would be a regular public vote with the least popular stars unceremoniously evicted. Yes, the very first series of *I'm A Celebrity Get Me Out Of Here!* was about to hit the screens.

With hindsight, it is easy to say that it was obvious that the show was going to be a monster smash. And in reality it did seem to have all the key ingredients that were winning huge ratings back then. It was also hoping to help the celebrities' charities raise plenty of money.

Even this final point failed to persuade Lorraine to join the likes of Tara Palmer-Tomkinson, Christine Hamilton, Nigel Benn and eventual winner Tony Blackburn down under when the show first aired. More than four years later, with the programme having pushed several contestants into the celebrity and financial stratosphere, it is not a decision she has ever regretted. 'I think if you give an outright "no" then they tend to leave you alone. I am very happy with my own level of just being reasonably well known, and wouldn't go on some other show to boost my profile to an extraordinary new level as I would hate not to be able to live my own life,' she said, desperately wishing that the very word 'celebrity' could be taken back to its original meaning. 'I am very aware that some celebrities don't seem to feel that they exist unless they see their names in the paper, but that's not me. There is not a barge pole in the world big enough for me to touch those kinds of show. Never, ever, would I do that,' she says of all the fame-led shows *I'm A Celebrity* has spawned.

Her career certainly didn't need any extra help. After some eighteen years on the breakfast sofas, Lorraine had actually turned herself into one of the best-connected women in showbusiness. From Hollywood legends to reality television wannabes there were few people she hadn't met or known. And there was very little about the fame game that passed her by. Her journalistic training made her a surprisingly good observer of human nature and the way the world worked. Gradually, the woman famous for being unremittingly nice was also building a reputation for being forensically honest.

Whether it was in her ongoing weekly column in *The Sun*, or in conversation with friends, she no longer took any prisoners when talking about her fellow celebs. 'It has to be said that the people who say fame means they can't lead an ordinary life are the ones who have made it that way themselves. I always say that if you don't want your picture taken, don't go to the Met Bar – go to the Dog and Duck. And if you don't want your fat face anywhere, don't turn up at a film première wearing something that resembles dental floss. Because you know what – if you do then they'll print your picture.'

She has similarly short shift for people who sell their wedding pictures to magazines. 'If you sell your wedding, then fine. But don't then get up on your hind legs and say your privacy has been invaded.' The woman who says that if forced to say she dislikes anyone would put bigots at the top of the list, says hypocrites are next in line. Anyway, she happily admits that when you do have a big enough name in the broadcasting world you hardly need to put up with the hassle of a big West End film première if you don't want to. 'Private screenings are one of the secret luxuries of my job,' she says. 'You can sit there with a cup of tea and a bun, and shout: "Projector man, can you turn it on now, please?" which is pretty wonderful.'

The source of Lorraine's surprisingly strident views on the unattractive excesses of today's 'celebrities' is easy to determine – it comes from her own eyes and ears. 'I have seen nice people in this business turn into monsters because they have not had the inner strength to resist believing their own publicity or because they have surrounded themselves with sycophants. So far, I think I have always had a sense of what is important and have kept my feet on the ground, something I think I have inherited from my parents.'

Back in Scotland, Anne and John were utterly proud of how well their only daughter was living her life. In fact, Anne is always on undercover duty to find out just how the wind is blowing and whether Lorraine needs to watch her back. 'If I'm in a shop and I hear people talking about Lorraine, I always listen,' she says. 'And everyone always has a good word to say about her. I never hear things like: "Who does that Lorraine Kelly think she is?" And I always resist the temptation to tell them that she's my daughter.'

In some ways it is actually Lorraine's family and friends who are keener on the high life than she is. Her mum has always been a huge film fan and loves the chance to go to the occasional film première and try some real-life star-spotting when she is in London. 'Lorraine has always got something lined up for me to attend,' says Anne, even though on most occasions her daughter gives the public part of the evening a miss and simply joins her later for a private dinner.

.This self-imposed purdah from the celebrity scene doesn't come about because Lorraine is a snob – the girl from the Gorbals could never be that. Nor does it show that she doesn't like mainstream entertainment – she says one of her key ambitions was to host *Stars In Their Eyes* and she was devastated when Cat Deeley got the job after Matthew Kelly stood down. Instead, her reticence simply stems from a very grounded perspective about her true role in life. 'I'm Rosie's mum, that's my real job. Being on television doesn't define me,' she says. And woe betide anyone wound up on the whole working-mum argument. 'I get really cross when people talk about working women, because I think all women work. My friend has got three under-five's at home – my life's a doddle compared to hers. All women run around like hamsters on wheels and if we allow ourselves to slow down at all we feel guilty about it. All mothers work.'

Having become increasingly open in her criticism of other people over the years, Lorraine is ready to be utterly honest about what she sees, sometimes, as her own shortcomings. On one occasion, when Rosie was just four and needed to have a scary injection at the doctor's Lorraine got caught in traffic and was too late to hold her hand as promised. 'Steve was with her but I should have been there too and that really hurt me,' she says quietly. She had long since vowed not to miss any of the precious moments in her daughter's life and she deeply regretted those that she did.

By the summer of 2002 she was ready for another professional challenge – she decided to defy public perception of her by appearing on the BBC's *Question Time*. The heavyweight show, hosted by David Dimbleby, is pretty much the jewel in the Beeb's political crown. Lorraine got mixed reviews for her performance. 'She wiped the floor with the politicians. Everything she said was common sense, and she was down to earth and funny as well,' said one viewer afterwards. Others were less kind about her practical wisdom, however. 'She applied the logic of *The People's Friend* to the Palestinian problem,' wrote a less sympathetic Scot. But at least Lorraine had tried. Once more, she had put her head above the parapet from where she could face some heavy sniping, and she hadn't for one moment felt out of place at the broadcast. 'Lorraine occupies a curious place among celebrities as a star of daytime television who can hold her own among politicians,' is how reporter Tom Lappin puts it. 'In all her guises she emerges as both approachable and intelligent, homespun and curiously worldly-wise.'

The bad news at this point was that her Sky TV adventure was coming to an end. The show itself was going well and the bosses at Sky were convinced it could have made real inroads into the daytime audiences. But when ITV Digital crashed, Sky lost a major outlet for the show. Viewing figures slumped towards the statistically invisible 100,000 mark, and on 31 May Lorraine and her team waved goodbye for the last time. There were none of the public tears that there had been at TV-am's demise, but with several crew members facing uncertain futures it was still a tough day for everyone to get through. Finding it increasingly difficult to sit still Lorraine soon found a new way to channel her energies – she became a regular guest presenter on the BBC Three's *Liquid News*, the cult daily entertainment news show, something of a coup for someone so closely associated with ITV.

That autumn she was also invited back on to *Have I Got News For You*, where she joined Germaine Greer as a panellist, with her old pal ITN's former political editor John Sergeant in the guest presenter's chair. But before and after this show went on air Lorraine was to make some surprising headlines.

The first came as she took her first steps – quite literally – towards becoming one of the country's biggest fund-raisers. After losing her gran to breast cancer back in 1991, she had always been looking for ways to raise money for cancer charities. In 2002, taking part in the Playtex Moonwalk seemed an ideal new way to do so. The Moonwalk is a night-time, 26-mile hike across London in aid of Breakthrough Breast Cancer and other charities. Several thousand women took part each year (the numbers have now swelled to more than 15,000 and include many men) and as she chatted away at the start line and en route, Lorraine found that almost all of them had been touched in some way by cancer. It was a humbling but inspiring experience, and the fact that everyone was encouraged to walk in a brightly coloured bra only added to the general camaraderie. Lorraine's bra, naturally, was tartan. 'It was for such a good cause I didn't mind if I looked silly. The only thing that wasn't fine was the toilet situation. I had to knock on the door of the Fire Brigade at one point and say: Let me in – I need to go!'

In the coming years, the Moonwalk would be an event Lorraine would move mountains to support. She continues to be one of its highest-profile supporters, making sure she is available to fund-raise for the London walks and the Edinburgh alternative she helped to push for. If this meant seeing unflattering pictures of herself tired and nearly topless in the papers, then so be it. She had long since given up worrying about what was written about her and treated most of her coverage as a bit of harmless fun – or at least that was how it was until the autumn of 2002.

15

SCANDAL

*'It was just a fun interview but all of a sudden
I was Ozzy Osbourne.'*

It all kicked off on an otherwise quiet, cold Sunday morning. Rosie was playing outside so Lorraine and Steve had temporarily reclaimed their sunny conservatory for a few moments with a cup of coffee and the Sunday papers. 'Steve and I have a little private joke,' says Lorraine of what happened next. 'Every Sunday, when we sit back read the papers, he'll say: "Oh, look, there's a picture of you in the paper." Usually it means there is a picture of a monkey somewhere, or something like that. And he does it every bloody Sunday. So when he said this one time that I was on the front page I said: "Aye, aye." And he said: "No, you really are. I think you might want to read it." And I looked and went: "Oh my God! Oh Jesus Christ!"'

It turned out that a racy interview Lorraine had given to gay magazine *Attitude* had been leaked to the tabloids – and, true to form, they had lifted the most salacious details and splashed them all over their front pages. 'Lorraine: I Took Sex Drug' was one of the banner headlines Steve passed to his wife that morning in their Berkshire conservatory. 'TV Lorraine's Outdoor Sex Romps' ran another. The articles themselves, spread over several inside pages, carried all the supposed details.

But as far as Lorraine was concerned it was all a huge storm in a teacup – as she told her agent and management company when they called to see if a damage limitation exercise was needed. 'I was asked hundreds of questions by this mad old queen and I was laughing my head off,' Lorraine says of the *Attitude* interview that had triggered the storm. 'Have you ever had sex outdoors?' was one of them. 'Once, but it was a long time ago. It was with my husband, in the hills of Scotland, and it was very nice but very cold,' was the gist of Lorraine's reply. 'Then he asked if I had ever tried poppers and I told him I had done once with my gay friend Gary, but it was like drinking nail polish remover and it made me go a bit loopy – so never again.'

But in those two answers the outdoor sex romps and sex drug stories were born. Could they be laughed off and dismissed as tomorrow's chip paper? Lorraine was convinced they could, and she was assured that GMTV bosses were taking them in their stride as well. Within a few days, she was able to really laugh about her sudden, and unexpected, notoriety. 'It was just a fun interview for a gay magazine but all of a sudden I was Ozzy Osbourne,' she told friends.

She was clearly something else as well: 'The most intriguing and unexpected gay icon of the past 30 years,' according to writer, social commentator and one-time lesbian Julie Burchill. Others had their tongues stuck firmly in their cheek when they tried to explain the phenomenon. 'Gay icons, as a breed, tend to have lived lives touched by tragedy and ludicrous excess, whereas ludicrous excess for Kelly probably amounts to a chocolate éclair with real dairy cream,' says her old school pal and reporter Allan Brown.

* * * * *

If her brush with infamy in the Sunday papers wasn't enough to prove how good a sense of humour Lorraine had, then two other people were about to put it to the test. They were presenters Ant and Dec. Lorraine and her team were working on an item about sugar daddies and had been over the moon to find two young women who were happy to come on the show and talk about their relationships with two pensioners. The old men were also happy to talk, and all four promised to be perfect guests. As usual, Lorraine chatted to the two women in the studio before the broadcast began to make sure everyone was feeling at ease. And as the show was underway she got ready to introduce the pensioners by video link to a rest home in Southend. As the men started to talk she flashed a quick glance at the monitors and around the studio. Something about all this wasn't quite ringing true. And then the joke was sprung. 'Kenny and George' weren't in Southend, they were in the studio next door. And they were, of course, Ant and Dec in heavy make-up for the latest spoof on *Saturday Night Takeaway*.

It made great television when the pair walked across to Lorraine and told her she had been had. And the day after the set-up was shown on *Takeaway*, the newspapers had even more digs at Lorraine's expense. 'So, Ant and Dec fooled Lorraine Kelly into doing something silly. Big deal. The real trick would have been to try and fool her into doing something sensible,' was how one unkind commentator saw it.

Making a fool of herself on her own morning show was one thing, but Lorraine's biggest fear in 2003 was that she might make a fool of herself on her next big evening appearance – when her usual modest ratings would swell to some two billion people. Fulfilling a lifetime's ambition, she had been picked to replace the long-standing announcer Colin Berry and read out the British votes at the *Eurovision Song Contest*. It was hardly a gruelling task, taking up less than three minutes of screen time, but with live links notorious for breaking down, Lorraine knew she would be a laughing stock if she missed her cues. Fortunately, everything worked well when Riga came calling, and Lorraine was on her way to becoming a big part of the Eurovision fabric. She went on to host the *Making Your Mind Up* shows to help pick future British entries and made her first foray on to BBC Digital when interviewing competitors during the big nights themselves.

* * * * *

At home in Berkshire, Lorraine sat back in her chair in her home office and looked at the huge pile of letters in front of her. Some she had brought home from the *Sun* (where her weekly comment page had been moved from Wednesday to the more prestigious Saturday edition), others had come via GMTV and yet more had somehow found her due to the sender's luck and the postman's good judgement.

As usual some of the letters were complimentary while others were angry – mostly criticising her for something she wrote or something she said or wore on television. But a large proportion of the postbag seemed to be asking for advice. Somehow Lorraine had become a de facto agony aunt, the final port of call for people with an extraordinary range of problems. 'People send her letters about their failing relationships, their failing diets, the gin bottle in their washing machine, anything, in fact,' said reporter Catherine Deveney, who took a look through the postbag with Lorraine in early 2003. Sending detailed individual replies was difficult, especially for the very personal letters where Lorraine would only know a fraction of the facts about a case. However, as certain themes began to emerge, she realised that more general advice might make a difference. So, as if she hadn't got enough to do, she researched, wrote and published *Lorraine Kelly's Real Life Solutions For Real People*. When she put the book together, she drew deeply on her own experiences, on the stories she had heard from guests on her television shows and on advice from family and friends. It would be practical, common-sense stuff, covering everything from relationships and careers to diets and body image for children.

The book got plenty of extra publicity late that spring when Lorraine found herself back on the front pages after a Janet Jackson-style 'wardrobe malfunction' of her own. It happened on 21 May, and she had just introduced her latest guests, a group of stars from *The Bill*. Everyone was chatting away and Lorraine remained blissfully unaware that her top was slowly slipping south, exposing ever more of her bra and her cleavage as it went.

In the programme's gallery the directors sat open-mouthed. No one was used to seeing quite this much of Lorraine, especially not at this time in the morning. The studio director grabbed the microphone and told her what was happening and the look on her face was pure comedy. 'Oh dear, my director has just told me in my earpiece to pull my top back up. I'm so sorry, I do apologise to the nation for that. I really didn't mean to expose myself,' she said, blushing, before ending up with a typical joke at her own expense. She turned to actress Trudie Goodwin, who plays Sgt June Ackland in *The Bill*. 'We were just talking about you being a strumpet and I'm a strumpet, too!' Viewers, though, were far from upset. 'I turned my television on as normal and thought to myself that Lorraine was wearing a funny sort of top. But as I hadn't been watching the show from the start I had no idea that it wasn't meant to be like that,' said twenty-eight-year-old Chris Weeks from Eastbourne, East Sussex, who was one of the many viewers the *Daily Mail* spoke to the next day about the incident. 'Luckily Lorraine is in very good shape for her age,' he added gallantly.

She didn't necessarily feel it on her next big GMTV assignment, however. *LK Live* was turned into *LK Does LA* for a week, with the star flown to California to report on the showbusiness and other trends out west. Her first task was to broadcast live from the Playboy mansion, where Hugh Heffner was charmingly complimentary about her. Looking at the tall, mostly blonde beauties all around her, Lorraine wasn't convinced he was being entirely truthful. 'I'm too old to become a bunny girl,' she admitted, as the crew moved on to their next location.

On her return to Britain she got a boost when one of the top 'lads' mags' suggested she was wrong to rule out the bunny-girl option. *Maxim* readers voted her one of the top 10 sexy older women in the world – and Lorraine was thrilled. 'How cool is that? The wee caption said: "Lorraine looks like she could show you a thing or two", which I thought was brilliant,' she said, laughing with friends.

On a more serious note, she was about to join a campaign

to promote one of her favourite hobbies: reading. Once more this would show the divide between the popular image of Lorraine as a breakfast television airhead with the reality of the intelligent woman within – she was going to take part in the BBC's *Big Read* project.

A close examination of her past shows she was an ideal choice for the role. 'I come from a family of bookworms and today my house is floor-to-ceiling books. The whole structure is groaning under the weight of them and I think the spare room is going to collapse,' she says. The books themselves are incredibly varied, a mix of popular favourites, such as Patricia Cornwell, Maeve Binchy and Ruth Rendell, to Dostoevsky's *Crime and Punishment*, which Lorraine describes as 'the best-thumbed book in the house.' Travel writer Colin Thubron is a recently discovered favourite along with anything written about Antarctica. She also laps up the books others may see as off-putting. 'I re-read *Crime and Punishment* recently because – well, just because, really,' she said in 2003. 'And when people say, "Ugh, I could never read *War and Peace*" they don't know what they are talking about. I stayed up until 6am last time I read it.'

People who are good with words are always her favourite companions, and she says Clive James and Peter Ustinov would join her husband and Elizabeth I as her dream dinner-party guests. As final proof of her literary worth, she revealed that as well as some moisturiser and an enormous box of chocolates, the third non-family item she would take to a desert island would be the complete works of Shakespeare. 'I could amuse myself for ages acting all the characters,' she said.

Her enduring love for Shakespeare comes largely from the way it was taught to her – by her favourite Claremont High

School teacher Miss McPhendran. 'She didn't just say: Write this down, because what is the bloody point in that? She led us to make our own conclusions, which I think is so important, especially when it comes to things like thinking about literature.' The same teacher also took the class to a special screening of Marlon Brando as Mark Antony when they were studying *Julius Caesar*. 'It certainly made an impression on the girls. I can't bear it when I hear people say: Oh, Shakespeare is so boring. And I think: How can these gory, passionate, amazing stories be boring?'

On *The Big Read* a group of well-known names were asked to champion favourite books. The idea was to encourage viewers to read them and then vote on the most popular. Lorraine joined fellow advocates who included William Hague, Clare Short, John Humphries, David Dimbleby, Simon Sharma and Sandi Toksvig. Her book of choice was Charlotte Brontë's *Jane Eyre* and she couldn't hide her enthusiasm. 'It's a fantastic book. The story just carries you off into another world. There is the mad woman in the attic and you can imagine the weather and all that thunder and lightening. It's just pure, pure, sexy passion and I love it,' was her key pitch to win votes from viewers. In the end Jane Eyre came tenth, however, with Tolkein's *Lord of the Rings* unveiled as the winner.

A sudden tragedy meant Lorraine wasn't able to focus on the final stages of *The Big Read,* however. In early December, her long-standing agent and friend Jimmy O'Reilly had a heart attack and died. He was just forty seven. 'He didn't smoke, wasn't a big drinker and had got to a stage in his life when he was really happy. I'm still in a state of shock and I can't believe it's happened,' said a devastated Lorraine when the news broke. She had spoken to him on the Sunday, the day before he died, and arranged to meet up with him on the Wednesday. In an awful, ghoulish coincidence, just hours after she had been told of Jimmy's death, there was a knock on the door at home. A big box with champagne and flowers had been delivered – Jimmy's birthday gift to her which he had arranged the day before his death.

'It was really upsetting. He was my agent, but to me he was more like my pal,' she said, working out they had known each other for some sixteen years and that he had represented her professionally for nearly twelve. Jimmy's passing would leave a big gap in her life for some time, and his death made her even more determined to focus only on the things in life that really mattered and to live each day as if it could be her last.

16

SPEAKING OUT

*'I've gone my own way, I've worn and
said what I like, and I'm still here.'*

Lorraine laughed like a drain when a friend went online
and found an unlikely anagram for her name – mix up
Lorraine Kelly and you get a Killer on Early. But sometimes
she admits she can live up to the description. 'I'm not Doris
Day and I have my moments,' she says of her darker side,
mentioning that her temper can be fiery and adding
mysteriously that she likens herself to a 'friendly tiger'. By
2004 these characteristics were displaying themselves in her
increasing willingness to speak out against people who upset
or offended her.

After criticising Liz Hurley three years earlier, Lorraine was
about to get involved in a spat with another model – the waif-
thin Jodie Kidd. The war of words began when Lorraine said
Jodie looked like a 'sick, anorexic giraffe'. Jodie hit back,
calling Lorraine a 'lowlife' and an 'evil cow' before Lorraine
tried to diffuse the situation by saying she had been talking
about Jodie's public image and her overall health, not her

looks or lifestyle. Her next set of targets were some of Hollywood's most famous names.

'We always laugh when the big stars come in,' she says of the GMTV experience. 'They've got loads of people with them and they're demanding this and that and the other. Well, our message is simple. We ain't got it: This is it, deal with it!' She said the arrival of the singer Shakira was a classic example. Lorraine said Shakira herself was a joy to meet. Her people, however, were not. First, they refused to accept the glass of water put on the table for the interview. Shakira, they said, needed her own water, and her own special glass. Lorraine just rolled her eyes and got on with her job.

'Usually, the bigger the entourage, the bigger the pain in the neck,' she says, remembering similar big-scale visits from the likes of Jennifer Lopez and Mariah Carey. 'The contrast is then so big with someone like Will Young, who just turns up on his own, does the show and goes home – a real pleasure.'

Back to Hollywood and Lorraine has other bones to pick. 'So many of the actors I meet have nothing to say – and when we talk it is like getting blood out of a stone. But Hollywood stars need to get real. You've made your film. Part of the contract is that you have to be put up in a luxury hotel suite and talk about yourself. How hard is that for an actor? It's not exactly asking for much, so you can at least look interested. They've a damned cheek to be bored.'

Lorraine being Lorraine, though, even her insults are rounded off with a little feel-good comment, a joke to sugar the pill. 'I remember when I interviewed Jennifer Lopez and afterwards thought, What was all that about? Because I had no idea. She sat there and said, Yes, I am in this place now where my inner child is, blah blah blah. Super bottom, though,' was Lorraine's considered opinion afterwards (leaving it to others to say that this was what Jennifer had been speaking out of).

Overall, Lorraine's serious side does worry about the way the wind is blowing in the celebrity world and the wider community. 'I think the country seems to have become harder since I started out on television, less nice,' she remarks in a rare reflective mood. 'Now we are often dealing with people who have behaved despicably but got away with it, become almost celebrated for it. People who have had affairs and who years ago would have been condemned for it. Now they make whole careers out of their affairs and become rich. The line between celebrity and notoriety is blurred and I feel sometimes as if we are going backwards.'

With this in mind, she admits that the thrill of meeting new and established stars is gradually wearing off. She finds herself far more impressed by the ordinary members of the public she meets on her shows, the ones pushed to do extraordinary things in their lives. 'I love a good human interest story about real people who have done something amazing more than chatting about showbiz stars,' she says.

What she didn't realise was that in 2004 her relaxed and chatty style was about to come in for more criticism than ever.

The London *Evening Standard*'s famously acerbic television reviewer Victor Lewis-Smith would lead the charge. 'With her unflappably friendly demeanour, her merry Scottish twang and her permanent rictus of a smile, Lorraine Kelly is increasingly easy to detest with every passing year,' he wrote. 'She agrees so readily with anything and everything her guests asset that she would doubtless say: "Och, Herr Himmler, I take your point about Zyclon B's advantages over Zyklon A," if so required.' Allan Brown, the old school-mate who had worked with Lorraine at the *East Kilbride News* and moved on to the *Sunday Times* was always there with some light-hearted ribbing as well. 'The fact that she has maintained a national career while speaking to every interview subject as though addressing a three-year-old child with a minor knee injury should be a fillip to us all. Prime Minister or soap star, it makes no difference to Lorraine: she just tilts her head, nods sympathetically and thinks of kittens chasing balls of wool,' he joked about her broadcasting style. 'Lorraine Kelly has basically earned vast amounts of money from telling celebrities how nice it is to see them,' said another commentator, as yet more critics lined up to have their say. Lorraine tried to ignore them all.

'I don't really care about the people who dismiss me for supposedly being fluffy,' she said, when asked about the latest onslaught. 'The people who say things like that are always the ones who don't actually watch the show and don't know what it is really all about. Yes, sometimes we will be doing something unbelievably fluffy – and there is nothing wrong in that – and then, for instance, I'll hear in my earpiece that they have just found the body of a little girl who drowned in France and you have to go straight to that item without making it crunch. It can be bedlam, bedlam, bedlam with the running order changing all the time but I say it doesn't matter. The viewers don't know all that. We have to put on a show that works.'

She also claims that she doesn't care if people are laughing at her rather than with her. 'The secret to it all is not taking yourself too seriously, which I don't. I'm not bothered if people are laughing at me. They're still being entertained and that's the business I'm in – entertainment.' There is a touch of steel in Lorraine as well, though, and it showed through when she tried to dismiss her critics once and for all. 'I've been presenting at GMTV since 1989 and I've gone my own way, and I've worn and said what I like, and I'm still here. That says it all.'

Even her legendary good humour and unexpected flashes of steel couldn't protect her when some of the critics moved on from the job she did on television and zeroed in on her appearance, though. 'Have you clocked Lorraine Kelly on GMTV lately? She's now even wider than Eamonn Holmes. Her head is like a football and her neck has disappeared,' wrote the far-from-slim Garry Bushell one Sunday in *The People*. 'Is Lorraine Kelly on Nina Myskow's diet? She's started to look like a blowfish in a Beatles' wig,' was his follow-up shortly afterwards. What he didn't know was that far from the public eye Lorraine was about to transform her body completely. Yes, she had let her exercise regime slip from her *Figure Happy* days and had fallen prey to a bit too much comfort eating, but she had found a way to tackle it. It was 26.2 miles long. At the age of forty-three Lorraine Kelly was about to run the first of her many marathons.

17

AND THEY'RE OFF!

*'When I crossed that finishing line I looked like a
mad old lady who had been run over by three or four trucks.
Everywhere hurt, even my hair was sore.'*

It was after a grey, wet week in Hawaii that Lorraine took
her first steps towards becoming a long distance runner.
She was on holiday with Steve and Rosie, and she was very
aware that she was failing her size 12 trouser test. 'It rained
every day and part of me was glad because I didn't have to
show my body. But you can't put your life on hold because of
your weight, and knowing that I was doing it was the spur
that made me try to eat better and get fit again.'

But what type of exercise would work for her on her return?

Fortunately, she reckoned she knew who would tell her.
Jenni Rivett was back in her native Australia but Lorraine
had met another fitness expert, Jane Wake, and the pair
had become friends. Jane was soon to become one of the key
experts on *Celebrity Fit Club* and while she approved of
the exercise regimes Lorraine had tried in the past, she
agreed that they had probably come to the end of their
natural lives. Jane's view is that most people ultimately reach

a point where exercise for its own sake isn't enough to keep motivation levels high: They need big goals to aim for, tough targets to hit.

The pair talked through a whole range of possible challenges for Lorraine before hitting on the idea of marathon running. Lorraine liked the fact that the training would have to be rigorous and that there was a fixed end date in mind at which she would find out if she had lived up to expectations. With family and friends knowing she was in a big race – let alone any fans who recognised her – she felt she would be under even more pressure to succeed. Like most marathon runners she relished the chance to get sponsorship and raise plenty of money for charity. A marathon it was, she decided, and she might as well start at the top with the London one.

The first person to notice the step change in Lorraine's life was Rocky, the family's border collie. His walks seemed to become a lot faster and longer. Running to Rosie's school before walking back with her daughter was another way Lorraine kept active. But the real challenges were new test runs she tried to build into her routine. There are no short cuts to marathon running, and Lorraine was determined to follow Jane's training schedule to the letter.

She started off doing two decent runs during the week, and then added in a monster every weekend. 'I reckon I have been exercising in total around six to seven hours a week, which is incredibly time-consuming. More than that, it's dull and I couldn't do it without Talk Radio.' As month followed month her other frequent companion was old pal Joyce, who was also planning to join Lorraine on the start line as another first-time runner – nervous London Marathon virgins, as they liked to call themselves.

By the time the big day came only the weather let everyone down. This was the year London offered the runners dark skies and driving rain, and Lorraine was feeling surprisingly nervous as the vast crowds waited for the starting gun. 'I'm more tortoise than hare, as you can tell. Put it this way, I don't think Paula Radcliffe has anything to worry about,' she said before setting off. But however slow she might be, Lorraine was determined to finish. Her uncle Robert had just had a triple bypass operation and much of her sponsorship money was going to the British Heart Foundation. She knew she had to make it to the finish line to do them proud. Plus, she wanted to prove the doubters wrong; all the people who said it was ridiculous that a middle-aged television presenter thought she could suddenly become an athlete. To her huge relief, she ran the race just as she had hoped finishing in five hours and 57 minutes, not a time that would bother the élite runners but not a bad result for a first-timer. And she still had enough energy left for some jokes.

'When I crossed that finishing line I looked like a mad old lady who had been run over by three or four trucks. Everywhere hurt, even my hair was sore.'

The following morning, at 8.35am, Lorraine was back in the GMTV studio as normal to talk about the event with fellow celebrity runner Nell McAndrew. 'It was galling that she was on the show with me because Nell didn't even break sweat and she got around in about three-and-a-half hours,' says Lorraine. 'Whereas I had to admit that I was only just ahead of that amazing ninety-three-year-old runner Fauja Singh – who I am convinced stood aside to let me go first.'

As Lorraine's blisters slowly healed, she was about to take part in a somewhat different race north of the border. While her weekday home was still in Berkshire she, Steve and Rosie were spending more and more weekends at their second home in Dundee and the university there was in need of a new rector. The role is both ceremonial and serious: the rector must promote and represent the university as well as hold regular surgeries for students to try and help sort out any problems. Former M15 agent David Shayler and Radio Scotland presenter Lesley Riddoch were her two main rivals and locals joked that Lorraine could hardly rely on fame to see her through. 'Most students won't know who she is or what she looks like – after all, her programme ends well before midday which is when most of those layabouts get up,' said one.

Others joked about how her daytime television persona would translate into academia if Lorraine did win the poll. 'Well, good morning! Lovely day, welcome! It's nice to see you all. We'll be cracking on with our lecture on quantum mechanics in just a minute but first, shall we have a chat about what's going on in the soaps?' was how the *Guardian*'s tongue-in-cheek education reporter Alice Wignall joked that the role could have panned out.

But Lorraine was serious about the task. It seemed an ideal way to put down even deeper roots in her adopted home town. As Britain's obsession with fame and reality television gathered pace, she also wanted to find a way to emphasise the importance of a good education. Just because she hadn't gone to university herself didn't mean she wasn't aware of how important the right courses could be, she said. The students agreed. She won 580 of the 866 votes cast, with David Shalyer coming second with 107.

Lorraine was thrilled. She was the university's tenth rector and the first woman to hold the post – something which meant a great deal to the feminist within her. 'The list of previous rectors includes the late and very much lamented Sir Peter Ustinov. I got to interview him very early in my career and he could not have been more charming to me. For my part, I intend to be a familiar face around the campus. I won't just be a figurehead,' she said.

The powers that be at Dundee were very happy with the choice. 'Lorraine has a cool head, a warm personality and plenty of versatility, which is important for the role,' said vice chancellor Sir Alan Langlands. 'She will be an excellent representative for Dundee,' added Student Association president Chris Bustin. Lorraine would certainly put Dundee on the map because there is a certain ritual involved in the new rector's appointment that she was more than happy to go along with. Most of it involved alcohol, and she proved she had the kind of stamina worthy of a student less than half her age. Her initial celebrations began with her sinking a pint of lager in the Trades House bar. The mum of one then downed a shot of absinthe in Popl Nero bar, before going on to the Braes pub, where she knocked back a local favourite called the Highland Coo, a mix of Drambuie, whisky and Baileys – and a straight double vodka! Amazingly enough, she still had the stamina for another lager before calling it quits. As part of the actual inauguration ceremony Lorraine then had to be dressed in ceremonial robes, sat in a carriage and dragged through the city by the women's rugby team. Surreal was hardly the word for it.

'I'm afraid I have been drinking absinthe so this might not come out right,' was how she began her first official speech after being installed as rector. 'What a day I've had! Being put in a carriage, dragged round the city centre and given free drink – I'm just delighted.' She was also slightly nervous about the next day, when she had agreed to present her GMTV show live from Dundee to celebrate and further promote the city and the university. 'I just hope my hangover is not too bad. I'll be drinking stacks of Irn-Bru – it always works for me after a heavy session,' she told the amazed students. Still game for a laugh, she also agreed to take part in a ten-point student checklist put together by the *Scottish Sun* to see if she really had what it takes to be a college kid. Her answers were typically funny.

'Can you down a pint in one go?' she was asked.
'Yes.'
'Do you like beans on toast?'
'Yes.'
'Have you ever been a communist?'
'For one week, so yes.'
'Do you say 'cool' a lot?'
'Yes.'
'Have you ever worn a traffic cone?'
'Yes.'
'Have you ever partied till the sun came up?'
'Yes.'

The two student-friendly activities she hadn't yet done were to dye her hair pink or fall asleep in a shopping trolley. She could only offer a 'Probably' to the ninth question – 'Can you burp and say "Scooby Doo" at the same time?' And she was forced to offer a: 'no' to the final student rite of passage – 'Do you lie in bed all morning watching Lorraine Kelly on television?' But seven out of ten seemed a pretty decent score for a mum of one, who had in reality gone straight from school to work at eighteen.

* * * * *

In London, GMTV bosses were over the moon about Lorraine's latest high profile among younger viewers and in the summer of 2004 they made her a big new job offer. Having made occasional appearances co-hosting *This Morning* for more than a year, it was announced that from September Lorraine would sit with Phillip Schofield on Mondays and Fridays when Fern Britton had her days off. She was euphoric. 'I'm excited because *This Morning* is such fun and Phillip is a joy to work with, he cracks me up. From the very first time I did *This Morning* last year he made me feel at home. He's such a lovely bloke and there's no ego, no nonsense about him. I've actually really missed having someone to sit with and bounce things off so the new role will be fantastic.'

Phillip was equally pleased to be working more frequently with Lorraine – he says he has never forgotten she was one of the first to text him with a complimentary message when he threw away his hair dye and appeared nervously on screen in his natural grey.

The new *This Morning* deal would confirm Lorraine's presence as one of the most popular, and therefore powerful, women in television. After twenty years in the business the *East Kilbride News* girl was still going strong. She was also still having fun. In one of her first shows as co-host the big medical slot was about a man who swore there are brilliant health benefits to drinking his own urine. So Lorraine and Phillip sat open-mouthed as he produced a glass, live on air, and proceeded to do just that.

'Don't do this at home,' said the show's doctor, Chris Steele, as Lorraine and Phillip tried to regain their composure.

That autumn, she was also going to show off her relaxed side again – agreeing that BBC Radio Scotland host Tam Cowan could broadcast his *Off The Ball* lunchtime show from her living room in Dundee. The producers say it was the first time they had ever done a show from someone's house and they were over the moon that she was game enough to give them the invitation. They also say their connection with Lorraine goes back a long way. 'She has turned out to be a big fan of the show over the years,' says Tam. During the phone-in one day they received a call from someone who was simply introduced as "Lorraine". The minute they heard the voice they guessed it was Lorraine Kelly. 'We had a bit of a banter with her and she told us that she would love to come on the show, so we have been trying to work something out ever since. The problem was that whenever Lorraine is in Scotland she is at her home in Dundee so it wasn't easy to get her to our Glasgow studio. In the end we thought it would be a good idea to take Mohammed to the mountain, so to speak. We've had all the stars on the show in the past – everyone from the First Minister to The Krankies. But it's the first time we've actually been in a celebrity's living room. It shows that Lorraine is really up for a good laugh and as long as she's got the tea and biscuits in, we should have a really good show.'

When the big day came Lorraine had to clear quite a lot of space – in addition to the full production crew a series of guests were due on the show that Saturday, including sports pundit Jim Spence. As well as providing house room (and tea and biscuits) she agreed to auction off one of her bras live on air to raise money for *Children In Need*. Martin Dowden, *Off*

The Ball's long-standing producer, became a big Lorraine fan in the run-up to the away day. 'She's been a really good sport the whole time we have been setting this up, and she has told me to insist that they don't hold back and give her a real ribbing on the show,' he said. So they did – mocking her over everything from her accent to her support of Dundee United.

Afterwards, it turned out that she had even more fans. 'You know how folk say that stars are never as nice in real life?' says outspoken sportswriter Bill Leckie, who had also been on the show. 'Well, in Lorraine's case they are dead right. Because she's nicer. Not an air, not a grace, she's plainly far happier surrounded by her old pals than by luvvies at the BAFTAS.' With a smile, he also confirmed she made a mean bacon roll.

Lorraine's next chance to spend a night surrounded by old pals came after she let slip on her show that as a schoolgirl she had had a secret crush on one of her teachers, Mr Somerville. Former classmates Miriam Moffat, Liz Mercer, Morven Vann and Sandra Seenan decided to arrange a big night out as a reunion. They booked a room at the Hilton East Kilbride – Lorraine admits she still can't believe that her old neighbourhood is now considered grand enough for a flash hotel – and started sending out invitations. She was one of the first to RSVP, and on the night itself she dressed up in a teacher's gown and mortar board to compère the quiz.

She took a deep breath before meeting Hamish Somerville, partly because she was nervous but partly because she was worried he would have been teased mercilessly since she had revealed her teenage crush to the world. 'As it turned out he was a cracking sport and it was absolutely brilliant to see him again,' she says. 'I also made sure his team won the quiz. It was a real night of nostalgia that began when I left my mum's house in East Kilbride and she warned me not to be late back – I felt about sixteen again! I can't thank everyone enough for giving me the chance to come along and hopefully we can do it again. It was wonderful to see so many familiar faces again.'

Many of the people at the party were old friends that Lorraine had never lost touch with over the years. But she says it was great to catch up with so many others who had moved away and were also back in town for a burst of nostalgia. For her part she was certainly not at the Hilton for some sort of half-hearted celebrity visit, working the room fast and leaving within moments of arriving. Instead she stayed at the bash for nearly four hours, and when the quiz was over she carried on dancing, joking and chatting until the very end. The reunion's organisers said it had been a brilliant event. 'Lorraine was very enthusiastic about the reunion from the start and it was great that she could come along. She flew back up to Scotland especially for the party and was really down to earth. There was plenty of banter going on all night. The quiz was brilliant and afterwards Lorraine said she just felt as if she was coming back for a big family wedding,' said Miriam Moffat.

Not everyone in Scotland was as happy with Lorraine that summer, though, because she had decided to wage a one-woman campaign against the new Scottish Parliament in Edinburgh. 'I am incensed by it,' she said of the building and everything it represented. 'I can't believe the level of the debate, and the amount of money they have spent on that building is shameful. How on earth can they justify spending £400 million? How can they not be embarrassed? I'd be absolutely mortified, I would be putting a paper bag over my head! At the Fraser inquiry I hate the way they are all going: "It was him, it was him," and pointing their fingers at all these dead people. The hypocrisy is astonishing.

'Billy Connolly calls it the "wee pretendy Parliament" and he's not wrong. I just see it as another level of bureaucracy that is costing us a fortune and actually isn't doing very much. I will never miss an opportunity to give it a kicking.'

In private, Lorraine joked with friends that she had found a good way to knock the Parliament building down – she could lean against it. Yes, with her marathon training over and the big race becoming a memory she felt herself piling on the pounds yet again. She was failing her trouser test and in danger of falling into the vicious circle of looking at herself in the mirror, not liking what she saw and then comfort eating, which only made matters worse.

Her first way out of the mess was slightly unconventional – she booked a Christmas holiday in Australia for the family and then forced herself to look at some holiday photos when she hadn't been at her best. 'In the pictures I thought I looked like Mr Blobby again. So this time I thought, on Christmas Day I'm not sitting on Manly Beach in Sydney in a kaftan. I wanted to be able to wear a pair of shorts, a top which showed my arms and to feel OK. So in September I cut out sweeties, biscuits, crisps and cakes. I filled up on fruit, vegetables and pasta. Basically I went back to my old rule: Eat less rubbish and get off my ass!'

The way she did this was just as unconventional as her motivation for doing so. Her next exercise regime would consist of cleaning – and sex. 'I am Monica, I've always been neat,' she says of the *Friends* character. 'I can't go to bed without making sure that everything's sorted. We have a lovely lassie who comes in on a Monday but through the week I do it all. Strangely enough I find it therapeutic to tidy up knicker drawers. I put Liberty X on full blast and dance while I dust. Vacuuming, ironing and hanging out the washing can all burn 100 calories.'

And that's not all – 'Good old-fashioned nookie gets the heart rate up as well. Fifteen minutes of active sex is worth 20 minutes in the gym.' And while sex with anyone but Steve was entirely out of the question, Lorraine was more than happy to follow the advice of her old favourite Joan Collins, who had famously made the point that: 'Just because you are on a diet doesn't mean you can't look at the menu.' So at the Scottish BAFTAS that year Lorraine found herself looking at little else. 'There's some top male totty here tonight,' she said in true ladette mode, as she checked out some of the local talent and giggled with her female friends.

More seriously, she had found another way to burn off her excess pounds. Marathon running had toned her up wonderfully, but she was still unsure if she could ever manage another big race. Power walking, though, seemed an ideal way to keep her trim and left her options open in case she did want to get really fit again in the future. She spoke to several experts and worked hard to get the walking technique right. Then off she went – and she loved it from the start. After less than three weeks she felt she had made real progress, though as usual she had to be tough on herself to stick to her schedule. 'Whenever I wonder how I am going to find the time to train, I remember that I manage to watch *Coronation Street* four times a week,' she says, with typical honesty.

So she made time for two or three long walks on weekdays, ideally with an even tougher, ten-mile trek at the weekends.

What she liked most about power walking was that with the right advice it was possible to lose weight where she wanted to the most. For Lorraine that meant her upper arms and thighs. The regime had other benefits, too. 'It clears my head, makes me feel invigorated because I know I've done something rather than just sitting around. I'm proud of myself for having done a big walk, and that's a precious feeling that I'd like more of us to share. I have more energy and I sleep better,' she said.

She was also ready to strut her stuff with the best of them at Manly Beach in Australia that Christmas – she felt slightly less voluptuous after the exercise campaign but was happy to report that her boobs were 'still hanging in there nicely'. In all she had managed to lose almost all her excess weight in less than three months, and once more people seemed to want more information on what she had been doing.

Another fitness DVD was on the cards, though Lorraine took a bit of persuading about whether to go through with it. The trend that year was for ever-tougher fitness programmes to be promoted – from military-style boot camp plans to extreme yoga courses, so would a routine based around walking get laughed out of the stores?

'Lorraine Kelly's exercise routine – walking. What next? Will she move up a level and tell us all how to breathe? Or maybe how to get out of bed?' was how one comic put it when her plans were announced. Fortunately for Lorraine, this was hardly the first time she had been mocked by the critics, so she had developed a pretty thick skin, and she genuinely felt her power-walking ideas had more relevance to the vast majority of women than those of the stick-thin Ashtanga yoga fans.

So *Walk Off The Pounds* hit the shops in time for the

Christmas and New Year market, and ultimately it won some surprising praise. The comics might not like it, but the fitness experts said it was realistic, sensible and – most importantly of all – achievable. In typical Lorraine Kelly style she had the final word. 'Exercising is really all about feeling and being healthier – losing weight is a bonus. When I wasn't exercising I felt like a battery hen, all I did was work, eat and sleep. That way you end up running on empty and you get old before your time. Who wants that?'

* * * * *

'Meet the stunning new Lorraine Kelly. Svelte, sassy and surprisingly sexy.'

Starting the New Year reading that kind of description is going to banish anyone's January blues. The compliments came care of an amazing photoshoot for *Top Santé* magazine that Lorraine posed for just before her Australian holiday. She had been persuaded to wear a little black dress with a plunging neckline and flowing hair extensions. 'The hair extensions are great and as for the dress – all I can say is that my husband is going to love it,' she told the photographers and stylists afterwards, with a big wink.

The feel-good factor would stay strong for a while. Fresh off the plane from Sydney, Lorraine hosted the 2004 Hogmanay celebrations and realised she was able to wear an almost identical Ben de Lisi dress to seventeen-year-old *Young Musician Of The Year* winner Nicola Benedetti. The only downside was that as Lorraine had been out on the streets interviewing revellers for much of the evening, she had been so swamped in coats and scarves that few people would have known how good she looked underneath. It was only when she was back in the studios, high above Prince's Street, that she got to show off her glam new look and dance away to the likes of Blondie and the Scissor Sisters playing in the gardens outside.

The fresh energy bursts she enjoyed from her power walking persuaded her to sign up to a whole host of new projects. She was still loving her GMTV shows but she wanted to broaden her horizons and take on other shows if they suited her ever-developing political, social and charitable conscience. The first to do just that was *Vote For Me*. The ITV show was widely derided as '*Pop Idol* for politicians', but Lorraine had high hopes that it would be a whole lot more. The idea was to create a new buzz about politics and to encourage people to take more interest in the way we are governed, a pet subject of hers for years.

The show began with filmed auditions for people who believed they had what it took to be an independent MP. Those chosen then came to London to be tested in various political tasks and grilled by the panel of judges. Viewers would then vote off the least convincing members before the winner was in a position to stand for Parliament for real. Lorraine was joined on the judging panel by former *Sun* editor Kelvin MacKenzie and former ITN political editor John Sergeant – one of her old pals in the political and media world. There was controversy from the start, however. Liberal Democrat culture spokesman Don Foster said he feared the show would be 'cheap and tawdry', while his Conservative equivalent was equally concerned. 'The danger is that this is either going to be a frivolous gimmick or crashingly dull. The temptation to go downmarket is huge and I have considerable misgivings,' he said.

Lorraine could also be forgiven for regretting her decision to take part after one bizarre episode on the audition trail. A contestant was to claim that she had grabbed her breasts – and spoke to the police about it. 'The woman was trying to get on the show to get prostitution legalised. She flashed her boobs then claimed Lorraine inadvertently brushed against her. It was in a room with eighty people. It is all on camera, no one was taking it seriously,' Lorraine's spokesman told the *Daily Mirror* afterwards. And while police confirmed that an allegation of sexual assault had been made, they said it was dismissed totally after the obligatory investigation.

Back at the *Vote For Me* studios (in the same building where GMTV was filmed), there was a general sense that Lorraine was on the panel in the 'good cop' role, with Kelvin MacKenzie expected to be the show's Simon Cowell figure. When filming began, however, she soon showed her steel. She didn't pull any punches when quizzing the hopeful MPs, determined to find out just how broad a knowledge they had, and just how much they cared about their biggest issues. 'Some of the candidates can hold their own under hostile fire – and surprisingly enough few were more hostile than Lorraine,' wrote critic Iain Weaver after watching the proceedings.

For all the high hopes of reawakening interest in government, *Vote For Me* was far from a success, though. It was shown over five successive nights, from 11pm, and on its first night it was beaten in the ratings by a repeat of *Men Behaving Badly* on BBC1. The winner – a right-wing ex-lawyer, who talked of deporting immigrants and castrating paedophiles – would pretty much disappear without trace. Having clearly favoured several of the other candidates for the winning position, Lorraine was forced to accept that the *Vote For Me* experiment had failed, but her personal quest to show that current affairs are just as important as the current favourite pop star or soap plot would continue.

In the spring of 2005, she found out that there was one thing she couldn't do for a career, and that was to make it as an artist. In her role as rector of Dundee University she was asked to join a long list of other big names trying to create an artistic masterpiece to promote the university. She wanted to make hers look good, but really she knew she would have to settle for making it look different, so she started off by painting the university's coat of arms on a white background and then scrawled 'Scotland's hottest' in wobbly letters across it, before sticking dozens of dried chillies around the edges.

Art expert Lee McCallum had his tongue firmly in his cheek when he gave his official verdict. 'Lorraine is undoubtedly one of the hottest rectors in the country and the juxtaposition between her art-work and her life are obviously inextricably entwined. The painting, unfortunately, was rubbish and left me, well, chilly,' he said, with a smile. Despite the negative critical reaction, Lorraine's untitled work still went on display at the university's Lamb Gallery, where the curators said it was the biggest draw in the room.

Sadness as well as pride touched her next major public appearance. After saying goodbye at the end of the day's *LK Today* show she was driven over the Thames to an anonymous-looking photographic studio near London's Regent's Park. The likes of Cherie Blair, Joan Bakewell, Jerry Hall, athlete Denise Lewis, writer and actress Meera Syal, and fellow presenters Denise Van Outen and Zoë Ball had all been gathering there since the early hours. All were there at the bidding of one man, the Oscar-nominated director Mike Leigh. His task was to film an extraordinarily moving advert for the charity Breast Cancer Care – the charity Lorraine had been supporting for nearly a decade. The nine women in the studio were all given the same short script to read on camera. Leigh would then edit it down so that each of them was seen reading just one sad line. Just like Lorraine, the other stars had personal connections with the charity, having lost friends, family members or loved ones to the disease. It was a sober, emotional, but rewarding day, and Lorraine was thinking of her late grandmother for most of it. As usual, she simply hoped that the promotions cancer charities did would encourage more people to watch out for the early warning signs of the disease and seek life-saving treatment before it was too late.

Working unpaid on projects like this was only one way that Lorraine felt she could help good causes. She knew the other was to raise money, and however much her feet, her body and even her hair had hurt after the 2004 London Marathon, she knew that few activities raised more cash than that. So, despite vowing she would never run another 26.2-mile course, she realised she would have to put her name down for the 2005 race.

'All the sponsors who hadn't quite made it in time for the 2004 Marathon were offering funds if I ran it again. It added up to between £30,000 and £40,000 for charity straightaway, so I knew I had to agree to do it,' she said, hugely pleased she had started power walking the previous autumn and got herself back into good shape towards the end of the year.

By the end of the winter Lorraine was training hard again, ignoring the rain and the cold, and pushing herself through up to three major runs a week – finding out in the process that there really is such a thing as the loneliness of the long-distance runner. Whenever she felt too tired, too stressed or too busy to head out and start pounding the pavements, she thought of the money she had been promised and the help it would do her chosen charities.

'Lorraine Kelly is not a quitter,' she swore to herself again and again as she faced what runners call 'the wall'. Having run through it she finally felt ready for the big day itself. 'I'm at the pasta phase, which is definitely my favourite bit of marathon preparation,' she said when one of the guests on her show asked how her training was going. She also let slip that she was running the one-mile Flora Family Marathon before the main event so that Steve and Rosie could enjoy the unique marathon atmosphere. 'An extra mile! As if I'm not crazy enough already,' she groaned with a smile.

18

A NEW DEAL

*'Fancy hitting Fifth Avenue and not
being able to buy any shoes!'*

Disaster nearly struck on the morning of Lorraine's second London Marathon. The rain and grey skies of 2004 had been replaced by near perfect conditions. But when she woke up she had a temperature, a scratchy throat and the beginnings of what felt like a particularly heavy cold. However lousy she felt, she knew she couldn't pull out – 'We had raised so much money for charity so I would have crawled if I'd had to.'

By the time she got to the crowded starting line she was beginning to feel better. Every runner says the atmosphere in London gets the adrenaline going and in a pre-run interview on the BBC Lorraine said she needed it more than ever in 2005. 'London is a fabulous city and it just comes alive for the Marathon. There's music, the crowds are shouting, pubs let you use their loo and children run out on to the course to give you sweets. I'd say the crowd ran about ten miles of it for me last year because they just kept egging me on to try and keep going towards the finishing line.'

For all this, it is wrong to take anything away from Lorraine herself. At forty-five years old the mum-of-one shook off her cold to finish her second full London Marathon, leaving herself just enough energy for a joke at her own expense. 'Did you see that? I was overtaken by three people dressed as Cornish pasties!' she screamed on GMTV, when she was shown a tape of her finish. 'It can be a bit soul destroying when Paula Radcliffe has finished the race, had enough time to do two poos, and you haven't even run ten miles! Nell McAndrew swanned over the line with an élite time of just over three hours, looking like a gazelle. I took twice as long and came over the line huffing and puffing and looking as if I had just been run over by a bus!'

A week later, Lorraine got up a little earlier than normal –as well as doing her *LK Today* show she wanted to be on the main GMTV sofa to wave Eamonn Holmes goodbye on his final show after twelve years. She was there with a selection of his other past and present co-hosts (though, unsurprisingly, not Anthea Turner) and Lorraine gave him a big kiss as the final moments of the show approached. Her double act with Eamonn had long since been eclipsed by his on-screen partnership with Fiona Phillips. But away from the cameras Lorraine and Eamonn had been closer friends than many might have thought. Most mornings in recent years he had been wrapping up his part of the show and preparing to leave just as she was arriving and getting ready to start, but she knew she would miss seeing him all the same.

One of the reasons for Eamonn's departure was his desire to spend more time with his growing family in Ireland. Seeing him achieve this goal made Lorraine wonder if she too could rearrange her working week to spend more time with hers.

Instead of doing five live shows a week, could she film three of them in advance, she wondered. That would allow her to spend up to five days out of every seven in Dundee, where the family was increasingly feeling at home. With lots of presenters' contracts up for renewal at this point she knew that this could be a good time to make the change. But she had to admit that there were problems. First of all she worried that *LK Today* wouldn't seem topical enough if more than half the weekly shows were pre-recorded in her afternoons off. Second, if she wanted to be away from London three days out of five then she knew all the presenters' days off on *This Morning* would have to be altered – and this was just too complicated to contemplate.

She and the bosses did reach a compromise, however. They would see how it went making three live shows a week and pre-recording the Tuesday and Wednesday slots. In return Lorraine would remain one of the best paid women on British television, collecting £250,000 a year for *LK Today* plus £150,000 for her two days a week co-hosting *This Morning*.

'I'm thrilled. I've got the best of both worlds, working in London and effectively living in Scotland,' she said when the contract negotiations drew to a close. The first big thing to happen to her after signing the deal was to face a typical Lorraine Kelly humiliation, however. One of her former schoolmates was on her show, the award-winning hairdresser Alan Edwards. It was the first time the pair had met since leaving East Kilbride and she made the hairdresser blush (while blushing just as deeply herself) by telling him how much she had once fancied his best friend David Devlin. The press, of course, were immediately on the case to track down this best friend and when they did, Lorraine was brought up short. David, apparently, didn't remember her at all. 'We seem to have been in the same places at the same time but I don't think our paths crossed. I don't really remember seeing Lorraine about or talking to her,' he told reporters with a laugh. His wife Margaret was equally happy to join the fun. 'I sent Lorraine an email with a photo of David and told her I understood her having a crush on him – after all she's only human. Everyone fancied David at school,' she said proudly.

The Devlins could get another look at Lorraine later that month when she entered the Dundee half marathon, saying she got a huge amount of support from the noisy local crowds who urged her on every step of the way. That summer, Lorraine was feeling particularly good about her body, her diet and her fitness. She hadn't stopped training after the London marathon because she had a big new goal in her sights – she, Joyce and a group of workers from the Highland Spring water company had put their names down for the New York Marathon as well. But the sight of Paula Radcliffe squatting down in the street to relieve herself after being caught short during the Athens Olympics had given Lorraine a new demon to slay before she could get out there and run.

'It's giving me nightmares because being caught short is something girls really worry about. I'd just die if it happened to me. I needed the toilet during the London Marathon but I went for a wee in a pub. I got a huge cheer as I came out of the loo. But New York is new territory for me and I have no idea if they will be as helpful. I should be worried about the training, the course or the weather, but all I can think about is: What will I do if I need a wee?'

Something else was bothering Lorraine as well as she prepared to head over the Atlantic. 'It's going to be really hard for me in New York, running down Fifth Avenue with all the shops shut. I mean, fancy hitting Fifth Avenue and not being able to buy any shoes!' As it turned out she survived both the Paula Radcliffe pit stop test and the shoe shop challenge but only after she and Joyce had once again been caught on the hop by the New York weather. 'It was so hot. I thought it was going to be freezing in November so I brought thermal undies, jumpers, scarves, the lot,' says Lorraine. 'But in the end it was in the 70s. We had to go out and buy suncream and sunglasses.'

The pair ran the race together, loving the bridge-crossing over into Manhattan and the final stretch through Central Park, where they brought a little bit of Scotland to New York by unveiling a huge Scottish flag over their heads as they crossed the finishing line together in just over six hours.

Lorraine's recovery from the race was to be a public affair – and would give rise to one of the funniest television moments of the year. She had one glass of celebratory bubbly, a brief nap and a few hours to try and recover before heading to a studio right on Times Square from where she presented her usual show live from New York. It was 2am in Manhattan and she says that after running 26 miles her body had no idea what was going on. 'The race has left every part of me aching. My feet are a disgrace and I am feeling very sore and giddy. But it has been the most fantastic run,' she told viewers.

To her credit, she certainly didn't look as if she had just run a marathon. Her hair and make-up was perfect (she says she always has to stop American stylists from slapping too much make-up on her face) and her clothes were suitably stylish. Overall, it was the perfect breakfast television look – or at least it was until she lifted up her feet from under the table and stretched them out on her sofa. All she could wear, she admitted, were the big white fluffy slippers from her hotel bedroom. The American crew said they simply couldn't imagine any of their own presenters having so much fun on air.

But Lorraine still didn't have much time to relax. With that first post-marathon broadcast out of the way she had to get a day-time flight back to Britain for her usual Tuesday show. By the time she was back it was becoming clear just how worthwhile the race had been. She had collected a huge amount of sponsorship in her own right, while her presence in the Highland Spring team seemed to boost their takings as well. The main charity to benefit was Breast Cancer Care, which was set to collect more than £200,000. Lorraine simply couldn't have been happier.

Her attitude to money has always been different to that of many of her fellow celebrities. Having been brought up in a household with little or no spare cash she always wanted to know there was a war chest of money set aside for a rainy day. She was also keen to make sure her daughter could have access to the best educational or other opportunities, should the need arise. But beyond that she admits that when it comes to spending she has no desire to keep up with the Jones's. As long as she and Steve can afford great holidays they are happy. Neither wears designer clothes or drives ridiculously flash cars. Both are constantly aware of how well they are rewarded compared to many of their friends.

But when it comes to charity, Lorraine thinks big. She had long since realised that her name could help good causes get a real lift, and that her efforts could transform their finances. So she had gradually turned into one of the biggest fund-raisers in the country. Her choice of charities is both broad and deep. Her marathons, for example, have raised cash for the Dundee-based Scottish Heart and Arterial Risk Prevention (SHARP) as well as for Maplewood School in High Wycombe, which helps profoundly disabled kids. She has also campaigned and raised funds to try and build a school for autistic children in Alloa, Scotland, as well as a hospice near Loch Lomond. The Multiple Sclerosis Society Scotland has enjoyed her help and she is also prepared to put her name to causes and issues that matter to her – however unfashionable they may be. 'Sometimes I will pick tiny charities which hardly get any money, so I want to do really well for them,' she says. In recent years she has tried to help everything from ChildLine, child literacy campaigns, anti-domestic abuse appeals and efforts to persuade Scottish women to become entrepreneurs. She has also encouraged more blood donors to come forward and led anti-bullying campaigns. When specific news stories or issues that mattered to her sprang up, she was ready to take action.

A key example came after the New York marathon when she read a survey showing that 63 per cent of teenage girls would rather be a topless model than a doctor or a nurse. The feminist in Lorraine was appalled, especially as she read on and found a quarter of young girls thought lap dancing was a good career while only three in a hundred wanted to be a teacher. Jordan, it turned out, was a dramatically more popular role model for fifteen to nineteen-year-olds than JK Rowling. Lorraine immediately agreed to stand alongside a host of fellow female achievers from writer Val McDermid to sportswoman Shirley Robertson to promote an 'Aim Higher' campaign created by the Scottish Girl Guides' movement to try and promote other forms of achievement.

Cancer charities, though, would always get her closest attention. She can never forget that her gran's illness was diagnosed too late for proper treatment. Back then, she feels there was an unnecessary but perhaps understandable taboo about talking about breast cancer. Today she wants to break this silence completely.

For Breast Cancer Awareness Week she is always ready to try and make headlines, using her usual no-nonsense style to persuade women to have regular checkups and spot any early warning signs. 'If you've got a man, get him to examine your breasts,' she said as part of that year's campaign. 'If you ask your man to check you over, what bloke is going to say: "Sorry, I'm watching the football." My husband Steve knows my boobs a hell of a lot better than I do. He certainly doesn't mind checking them over now and then.' Yes, that kind of comment might be a bit racy for some, but Lorraine's belief is that if it persuades just one woman to start regular checkups that could save her life then it was worth it.

What made her particularly proud in 2005 was the fact that her endless fund-raising had somehow been noticed. In the promotional efforts of The Year Of The Volunteer several thousand Brits were polled to see which famous names were most likely to persuade them to give time or money to charity. *Live Aid* and *Comic Relief* giants Bob Geldof and Lenny Henry were named the top two, but Lorraine was thrilled to see her own name in the top ten, ahead even of kids' role model David Beckham.

* * * * *

On the work front she was as busy as ever when 2005 drew to a close. And as far as their home was concerned she and

Steve had big plans for the following year. They had decided to sell up in Berkshire and move back to Scotland for good. Both would miss their southern friends and neighbours, as of course would Rosie. She had become firm friends with Ulrika Jonsson's son Cameron and Carol Vorderman's daughter Katie. 'Rosie will be watching telly and she will suddenly say: "Oh look, there's Katie's mummy on the telly" or "There's Cameron's mummy on TV". She thinks every mum is on the television,' Lorraine laughed. But their lives weren't lived entirely amidst the famous names of their adopted country. Lorraine was now a big part of the Parent Teachers' Association at Rosie's school, Steve was in a local five-a-side football team and they all felt utterly happy in their little community. 'We don't have a glitzy lifestyle – it's very normal where we live. People stop me in the supermarket and say they are surprised I do my own shopping. But who else is going to do it? I clean my own toilet as well.'

Giving all this up was going to be a wrench, but Rosie was about to leave her primary school and it seemed to make sense to be established in Scotland in time for her new life in secondary school. So, after some sixteen years down south Lorraine sold up in Berkshire, enjoying a huge profit on their massively extended home. Dundee was the obvious choice for their new base. Steve had his roots there and Lorraine had fallen in love with the city just as she had fallen in love with him. It was also close enough for her parents to make regular visits.

Deciding that the holiday home they had loved there for so long wouldn't be big enough as a full-time base they started calling some estate agents. After looking at more than a dozen properties around the city the family settled on a £750,000 house set in several acres of land on the banks of the River Isla. Rosie was enrolled in a local secondary school just in time for the new term and Lorraine started to put a brave face on her long journey to work. 'Commuting is hard but if I'm going to travel to work I might as well do it from Scotland as from Berkshire,' she said at first, knowing few people would actually believe her. But after a while she had the facts to back it up. If things went well then the short hop from Dundee to City Airport in London needn't take much longer than the traffic-delayed trip up the M4 from her old home.

The problem, of course, is that things didn't always go well.

In October 2005, Lorraine climbed aboard the tiny Dornier 328 plane in the early morning as usual for the one-and-a-half-hour trip down south. But a series of long delays meant the plane remained on the tarmac for nearly an hour longer than normal and then got held up again in the rush to land in London. As she had called the GMTV production team as soon as the first delay was announced, Lorraine knew they would have pulled out all the stops to get her through the London traffic when she did land. What she didn't know was that this would involve her being handed a full set of leathers to wear before she was sat on the back of a motorbike and whizzed through Docklands to the South Bank. Motorbike taxis were the latest gimmick among city executives, with fans saying they could easily beat black cabs and any other form of transport. But they were a first for Lorraine, and she clung on for dear life as her driver weaved through the cars and screeched to a halt at her studios. Phillip Schofield thought it was hilarious. He had been due to co-host *This Morning* with Lorraine that day and was keeping viewers fully up to date with her progress. 'They have whisked Lorraine across London on a bike and they are now trying to tame her hair in the make-up room,' he joked, after fronting the show solo for forty minutes.

'Philip, I'm so sorry. Are you alright?' Those were Lorraine's first words as she finally rushed on to the set, to a rare ripple of applause from the camera crew. 'I was asking the pilot if he would just give me a parachute as we came over London but he said no.'

Fortunately, early starts and occasional late arrivals weren't going to take the shine off her new home – and she was quick to talk up the new life she and her family were building up north. 'I do just love Dundee – settling here has definitely been one of my best moves.' She had noticed an astonishing number of changes in the past ten years and felt a new confidence in the city. 'It's a cracking place to live. It has been hard for people there to get over what happened in the 1970s and there is still this prejudice among people who have never been there but it's thriving; it's got this great cultural buzz about it. I'm proud of it, passionate about it. I feel like an adopted Dundonian and I get very cross when other people have a pop at it.'

She was also happy to turn her house into a mini-tourist attraction for a while. It began on her first birthday back in Scotland when Steve, as usual, was stuck for a gift idea. Lorraine admits she is a nightmare to buy for because she has so little interest in the obvious gifts like clothes or jewellery. Suddenly, Steve had a flash of inspiration. Every time the family went for days out at the local science centre in the city Lorraine commented on how much she liked the four penguin statues outside the building. So Steve tracked down the name of the artist who had made them – Tim Chalk – and asked for a 4ft 6in model of his own to give to his wife.

'It was a stroke of genius,' Lorraine said, proudly putting the statue in the front garden of their Dundee home and even rigging up a purple light to show it off at night. 'People out walking their dogs get a bit of a shock but it seems to make everyone smile. We put a scarf and hat on him in the winter and in the summer we are going to get him some sunglasses.' Fortunately, the neighbours loved it as well. 'It has become a minor tourist attraction with people coming along and taking photographs,' said retired ship's captain Steve McCarthy. 'It has certainly added a bit of humour to the place.'

* * * * *

At work no one was laughing about Lorraine's next job, however. The woman who was so often derided for playing safe in her diets and makeover comfort zone had decided to work on an utterly controversial new idea for the evenings. It was born partly out of her own geeky love of sci-fi. The girl who sat with her dad watching *Star Trek* had kept up with scientific trends ever since. Now she was fascinated by the latest advances in DNA testing. The result was the idea for a show – *Secrets Revealed – DNA Stories*. The idea was to cover all sorts of relevant issues, but Lorraine and the producers were very aware that paternity questions were likely to dominate the show. Is your father who you think he is? Is your brother really your brother? Have you got more in common with your best friend than you might think? In the pilot show the plan was to examine the participant's stories using reconstructions while the DNA testing went on in the background. When the results were revealed the show would follow just how big an effect this might have on the participants' lives.

Obviously, everyone was very aware that this was sensitive ground. Lorraine in particular, wanted to put plenty of safeguards and support networks in place – this wasn't to be some kind of American-inspired trailer trash TV. 'Obviously when people are told the outcome of their suspicions it can be a life-changing moment,' she said when the critics told her she was in danger of crossing a line with the show. 'So we follow that with counselling and expert help. I couldn't do it if I was leaving people thunderstruck and floundering over what to do next. I'm not about to shatter someone's life and then move on.' Her focus, she said, would be on the aftermath of the test results and the way they can finally lay old ghosts to rest and help people move on with their lives on more of an even keel.

Critics of the idea were not convinced, however. The idea of *Secrets Revealed* simply seemed too insensitive. And when volunteers to come on the show proved hard to find the idea was quietly dropped. Like *Mum's The Word,* an ill-fated dating show that had been cancelled amid similar worries over its suitability, Lorraine's reputation was deemed too important to be wasted on what could be condemned as trash TV.

One good thing to came out of the show's early demise was that her diary was suddenly clear, so she was able to agree to two long-standing offers from two quite different sets of production companies. The first came from Hat Trick Productions, makers of *Have I Got News For You.* After two successful appearances on the panel, the producers had been trying to persuade Lorraine to appear as a guest presenter. Now she finally had the time, but she admits that as the big day approached she started to regret it. If she had been nervous as a panellist, she says, this was nothing to the butterflies in her stomach when she had to hold the show together and single-handedly keep Paul Merton and Ian Hislop in check.

'When the music started I thought, who do you think you are kidding, girl? Who do you think you are? And I couldn't remember when I had been more nervous.' Crew members at Hat Trick say she had no problems holding her own, on and off camera, and put her on the list for a repeat stint as soon as possible.

The next event she finally had time to sign up for promised to offer more fun and a completely different type of stress. Over the years she has made cameo appearances on everything from *The Bill* to *Brookside* and has never hidden her love of *Coronation Street* (her favourite *Street* character, Hayley, recorded a special birthday greeting for Lorraine outside the Rovers Return for her fortieth birthday). But Lorraine says a little-known Scottish soap often beats its rivals for dramatic and comic storylines. It is *River City* and Lorraine says she has never understood why it isn't broadcast south of the border. 'You've got *Coronation Street* set in Manchester, *Emmerdale* set in Yorkshire, so why not *River City* set in Scotland? The quality of the show, the acting and the storylines mean it could easily compete with the other soaps and give them a run for their money. There is absolutely no reason why it shouldn't be shown across the whole network,' she said, endlessly referring to the soap in her newspaper columns, on GMTV and in interviews.

Maybe getting a walk-on part would lift its profile enough to make the leap, she thought. The original idea was for Lorraine to appear as an old pal of salon owner Billie Davies. She would be in the crowd scenes at the wedding of Gina Rossi and Archie Buchanan filmed as part of a one-hour special. But she had a wish of her own and after talking it over with her mum, another huge fan of the show, she asked if her character could somehow get to meet their big hero, Shellsuit Bob, played by twenty-two-year-old Stephen Purdon. The producers and writers agreed straightaway and then decided they could go one better. They wrote in an extra scene so Lorraine could not just meet the fictional Bob Adams but get a smacker of a kiss from him as well.

On the first of the two-day shoot deep in an industrial estate in Dumbarton, Lorraine was fitted out with a cardigan the colour of tomato soup, a cleavage-boosting flowery dress and a pair of matching shoes – with felt attached to the heels to stop them clicking when she walked across the set. What she felt she really needed though was some way to stop her knees from knocking – she was shockingly nervous. 'I'm partly scared because it is like going through the looking glass. I feel as if I know everyone, although of course I don't, and it is very difficult not to call everyone by their character's name.' The original idea was for her mum to be there to hold her hand – the producers had written in a part for her as well – but she had got a heavy cold just days before filming. 'She is gutted to miss it, but she knows she wouldn't be very popular if she gave the whole cast a cold,' Lorraine said, as she turned up alone.

As expected, everyone worked hard but had a great first day on the set with their celebrity guest. And the high point was the big kiss with Shellsuit Bob. 'I won't wash again!' Lorraine screamed at the cast when the cameras had stopped rolling, then immediately made them laugh by asking if there was any chance of a retake – or six.

'Stephen is a wee darling, I want to wrap him up and take him home in my pocket,' she said, embarrassing the young actor even further. 'I'm still blushing over our kiss.' When he recovered his poise Stephen was equally complimentary of his new co-star. 'The set was buzzing and everyone was really looking forward to Lorraine coming in. She's a real icon in the entertainment world and it was great to get her on the show. For me it was just good to meet her in the flesh, let alone to plant a kiss.' He also said she was surprisingly good at her job – getting all her lines and moves right first time. 'We're thinking of asking our bosses to bring her back again because when she was here we finished filming early as she was word perfect every time,' he said.

'So, what is it like playing yourself in a soap?' reporters asked at the press conference after the filming.

'It is a big stretch. It will be the Oscars for me next,' she joked with typical self-deprecation.

Jokes apart, Lorraine said the chance to be in *River City* really had meant a lot to her. She kept her script with her lines highlighted in yellow as a souvenir and asked the whole cast to sign it before she left the set. As she did so, there was indeed talk of a film role – industry rumour said she would star with fellow Scot James Cosmo in an animated film called *Secret Realm*. The story follows the adventures of a lad called Stuart, with Lorraine playing his mother, Heather. A firm start date wasn't agreed, however, and she admitted that she wasn't ideally suited to acting. 'I could never do this as a job,' she said after the *River City* role, admitting that she had suffered an extra burst of stage fright before the cameras started to roll. Learning her lines had also been far harder than she had ever imagined. At home Rosie played all the other characters day after day, while her mum tried to remember her cues and stop ad-libbing as she always did on her live broadcasts.

When her soap appearance was shown, Steve said he wanted to buy his wife a gift to say congratulations. But, as he was well aware, Lorraine is incredibly difficult to buy for. With annual earnings well above the £400,000 mark she is both one of the highest paid, yet somehow most down-to-earth women in television – the one you can truly believe when she says she simply doesn't see the point in owning flashy clothes or jewellery. When her mum once gave her some Armani earrings for Christmas she wore them so often that her GMTV colleagues started to joke that she must sleep in them. 'Instead of expensive objects I prefer to just keep lots of items that are special to me,' she says. These include the sprig of heather her father wore as a buttonhole at her wedding and the glass vase her make-up artist and friend Brenda gave her as a wedding present. 'I'm a nightmare to buy presents for, so people tend to buy me flowers and chocolates – though with Steve I am always dropping hints for something ridiculous like a holiday in Alaska. When it comes to my own money I tend to spend it mainly on travelling and plants for my garden. When I hear about celebrities spending, say, £100,000 on a necklace I just think how many great holidays you could get for that money.'

That's perhaps why holidays and adventures are the first thing she thinks about when she is buying gifts for others. She gave her mum and dad a dream trip on Concorde for her father's fiftieth birthday. 'Money can make you comfortable, it can make you miserable, but I don't think it can make you happy,' she says. In many ways she focuses on giving it away as much as earning it. She calls herself a 'huge' tipper, not least because she remembers what it is like to rely on that kind of cash. 'I've had the 10 pence tips, where you just think, Oh, here, have it back you miserable git!' Now, depending on service, she says she will leave 15 per cent and sometimes 20 per cent on the table.

* * * * *

As 2006 got underway Lorraine was once again planning to shock a few of her more conservative fans. Having laughed like a drain throughout most of her appearance on the Graham Norton's chat show two years earlier, she now agreed to be guest co-host on the latest show in Channel 4's Friday night comedy slot. The jokes she cracked on the very adult *Friday Night Project* with racy comedians Alan Carr and Justin Lee Collins would have shocked those who were still blinded by her long-standing mumsy image from breakfast TV. But anyone who actually watched her on *LK Live* or *This Morning* would know that some earthy humour is normally just below the surface. Not for nothing do the tabloids often refer to her as 'saucy telly queen Lorraine' – a description she says was only beaten when the *Daily Star* once introduced her in an article as 'busty telly stunner Lorraine Kelly'. She might be one of the country's most famous middle-aged mothers, but Lorraine was still ready to spring some surprises.

19

FLIRTING

*'I can't believe it. I've been beaten by
a cartoon character!'*

L orraine clamped her hand to her mouth and started to
giggle. 'Oh my!' was all she could say as the *This Morning*
programme got underway, leaving Phillip Schofield to explain
what was going on.

'A man off camera is completely naked. Let's have a little
professionalism here,' he joked to Lorraine as the guest
dropped his towel, and climbed on to the massage table for an
all-over wax. Lorraine, though, was still having fun. 'Easy
tiger,' she said when the model rolled over on to his back to
have his chest hair removed – with just a small white towel
protecting his modesty. Later she was asked to run her fingers
through the chest hair of a different male model to compare
'before and after' sensations. 'I've got the best job in London,'
she laughed, as the item came to an end.

There were similar laughs on a subsequent episode of *LK Live*.

'I've got a side-on view. And let me tell you, the side-on view
is fantastic,' she said, amid her usual giggles when three male

models were parading around the studio showing off the latest underwear ranges.

A few months later, when the studio discussion was about a herbal so-called 'love pill', Lorraine was feeling equally mischievous. 'Be afraid. My husband's away,' she quipped to the crew, as she swallowed one and waited to see what happened. Her support for *Pop Idol* contestant Darius Dinesh brought some similar sexual tensions to the set. When he had been in the final ten of the first series she had jokingly opened her suit jacket on GMTV to reveal a tight white T-shirt with the words 'Vote Darius' emblazoned across her chest.

When he didn't win the contest and then launched his first single he stayed in the news, not least because of one infamous photograph. He was singing on stage in Scotland and inadvertently proving he was a true Scotsman with nothing on underneath his kilt. Within days the picture had become one of the most swapped images on the internet. When he came on Lorraine's show, Darius should, perhaps, have expected her to comment on it.

'Have you seen the photo?' he asked her, clearly embarrassed.

'Seen it? It's my screen-saver!' she told him as he put his head in his hands.

'Lorraine, quite simply, is one of the most flirtatious women on television,' says critic Sandy Eady – and her guests seemed to love it. Bruce Willis, for example, left her unusually flustered when he told viewers how sexy he found her accent at the end of their 2005 interview. Paul Gascoigne went even further.

'Give us your email address and I'm sure me and you can get a little something going,' was Gazza's suggestion, mid-interview, though at first he didn't seem to be getting through.

'I heard that ... but Lorraine ignored that, didn't she?' co-host Tris Payne interrupted as Lorraine tried to move swiftly on.

'I know – I just let that one go right over my head,' she said.

'Yeah, you didn't listen to it. That's like many women nowadays,' Gazza concluded with a wry smile – though he wasn't yet ready to give up. The producers had dredged up two video clips for the show, one of Gazza singing 'Fog On The Tyne' and the other of Lorraine's spoof version of The Proclaimers' song '500 Miles' from *The Frank Skinner Show*.

'Maybe we could do a charity single together?' he asked.

'You know what, anything could happen,' she replied, not entirely sure that it would raise very much cash. Her next admirer was Will Young. 'I want to go on a pub crawl with you, I want to go to Dundee. I think you'd be a laugh,' the *Pop Idol* winner said before she had even begun their interview. And Lorraine was forced to admit that the idea of a big night out wasn't exactly out of the question. 'I went on a pub crawl on Friday. I ended up at a bar called Fat Sam's, I think. I was the oldest one there. So we could go out, it would be great fun,' she told him.

Hollywood actor Robert Downey Jr raised the flirtation stakes to their maximum level a couple of months later, however. 'Hi, you look really well,' Lorraine said as she welcomed her guest as usual.

'Thanks. I was going to say that your tits look great too – particularly today,' he replied, leaving her totally and unexpectedly speechless. It seemed as if the still-popular Lorraine Kelly Appreciation Society had a new fan – and Lorraine's chest was as high profile as ever.

Her cleavage made the headlines again the previous month

when she dropped a paper fan down her front during *This Morning*. 'Look somewhere else,' Phillip Schofield had told the cameramen (to no avail) as he leapt forward to try and fish it out while Lorraine's famous giggle drowned out all other sounds. 'There can't be another presenter on daytime TV who has her thrupennies on show quite as much or as often as Lorraine,' joked the *Sunday Mirror*'s Carole Malone afterwards. 'She might have built her reputation as the girl next door but the fact remains her bosoms have had almost as much exposure as Jordan's.'

They were perhaps the reason why she was so popular among adolescent and twenty-something men, although not all the news from this area was good. Just after the Robert Downey Jr incident, *Nuts* magazine announced the result of its unique WISF Survey (the initials stood for Women I Secretly Fancy). And the top of the chart came Lorraine, just ahead of DJ Jo Whiley and property expert Sarah Beeney. One in reader in three said they fancied Lorraine, but wouldn't admit it to their mates – and the reason for the secrecy was the sting in the tail. Why keep it secret? 'In case their friends say: What? Her? But she looks like a farmer in a dress,' was how the magazine put it, with typical bluntness.

Fortunately, Lorraine was able to see the funny side. Just as she did when it was announced that she had come second in the Best Mother in Public Life poll for the Mother's Union. The winner, amazingly, was Marge Simpson, which created a huge amount of hilarity in the Kelly household. 'I can't believe it, I've been beaten by a cartoon character!' Lorraine wailed to her husband and daughter when they were told of the result.

* * * * *

As it turned out the *Nuts* and Mother's Union polls were only the precursor to a far more important accolade. It would come in Lorraine's twenty-first year on screen, in itself an incredible achievement in an industry famous for chewing up talent and spitting it out as soon as a younger model came along. Female presenters including Selina Scott and Anna Ford had frequently said that television has no role for women in their middle age and beyond. So were they right? Sometimes Lorraine worried they might be. 'I've always been aware that I can't do telly forever. It's a bit like being a footballer – it's fantastic but it has a finite life span and the moment the viewers don't like you, it's time to go, and of course that day will come for me,' she said, after passing that twenty-one year milestone. But the industry itself seemed to disagree. Her broadcasting life span was about to be given an indefinite extension because she was about to win an extraordinary accolade.

On 14 March 2006 she was named Best Presenter in the prestigious Royal Television Society Awards, effectively the 'Oscars' of the UK television industry. Earlier in the evening at London's Grosvenor House Hotel had seen the likes of Paul O'Grady and Catherine Tate win awards, alongside the production teams of the BBC's *Bleak House* and the documentaries *Holocaust* and *Children of Beslan*. It was the very best of company to be in and Lorraine had been thrilled just to be nominated. 'I nearly fell off my chair, it's the most surprising thing that has ever happened to me,' she said when her name was announced as the winner. But she shouldn't have been. The awards were set up to recognise television presenters who are at the top of their game, those with total command of the medium. Put like that, you can see why it had to be Lorraine. 'Versatile, entertaining and professional – the Breakfast Queen is unwaveringly warm,' said the judges as they explained the reasons for her triumph. Her fellow nominees were also ready to praise her – even if they did so with their tongues firmly in cheek. One of the men she beat to the award was Jeremy Clarkson, and he said he couldn't begin to compete with her. 'I couldn't interview the people she does without hitting them over the head with my shoes,' he joked.

As she made room for her award back in Dundee, Lorraine found out she was on something of a roll. She was named Celebrity Mum of the Year at a ceremony at London's Waldorf Hotel – sweet revenge on Marge Simpson she joked with her family afterwards. More seriously, though, Lorraine wanted the media to focus on the other women at that glittering awards ceremony. The so-called 'ordinary' mums who had overcome extraordinary challenges to raise their families. 'I'm really pleased with my award but the other mothers here are the true heroes. I feel terribly inadequate compared to all these other amazing women. What they have all overcome is amazing,' she told the press afterwards.

Among the other guests and winners was cancer sufferer and former nurse Barbara Clark, who got a special recognition award for fighting for wider availability of the breast cancer drug Herceptin. The day's overall Mum of the Year winner was Suffolk-based Carole Hall, aged forty six, who has fostered more than three hundred children over the past sixteen years. 'When kids come to you so distressed at what has happened to them and then they leave your house and you have made them smile, that's the joy,' she told Lorraine and the other guests of her role. Talking at length to

Carole confirmed Lorraine's belief that offering help to unloved kids would one day be a big part of her own future as well.

More than five years after her miscarriage she and Steve had accepted that their little trio of a family was never to get any bigger. Lorraine says that like many women – including the countless ladies she had interviewed on her shows over the years – she had briefly considered fertility treatment to give nature a helping hand. But in many ways, talking to all these other women had made her hold back. She remembered so many stories she had been told, some with a smile, others told through tears. The women with no children who were desperate to start a family, those who wanted a bigger family, or whose existing child or children had tragically died, the ones who couldn't afford or didn't qualify for IVF, the ones for whom it simply hadn't worked. Lorraine felt she had learned something from all of them. 'I realised that I didn't feel so overwhelmed about it that I wanted to have fertility treatment myself. Steve and I would have loved to have had more children. But we just tried it in the old-fashioned way and it didn't happen. Sometimes it is not to be and we have accepted that. Now I am too old. I am just so glad I was able to have one healthy child,' she said. Subject closed and time to move on – or was it?

A couple of years earlier, Lorraine and Steve had filmed a series on adoption for the BBC called *A Family Of My Own*. Neither had ever really forgotten it. 'The show was tough to do. It was both heartbreaking and inspirational. Some of those kids overcame so much, some of their backgrounds were so horrific,' Lorraine's voice tails off as she thinks back. Ever since, at the back of her mind was the idea of returning to this subject in the future. Maybe she could do more than simply highlight the issue of adoption, fostering and supportive lodging with charity work and a television documentary. Perhaps she should get involved at the sharp end by joining the band of volunteers who open up their homes to disadvantaged children. The woman whose sense of social justice had always told her that those who have should offer something to those who don't was acutely aware of the opportunity here. The idea of providing a stepping stone to kids in care who are about to go out into the world for the first time as adults was hugely challenging, but it felt totally right. The only problem was the fear that living in the home of a 'celebrity' foster mother, even for a short period, might mean the kids were forced to live a vital stage of their lives in the spotlight. The paparazzi have never been a problem for Lorraine or her family. She has never courted photographers, never paraded herself, Steve or Rosie in front of them, and never been the centre of any scandal that would encourage them to follow her. But she felt she couldn't rely on this state of play continuing forever. When she and Steve considered the practicalities of fostering or offering respite care they knew it probably wouldn't work while she was still appearing on television. But the idea was filed away for the future, a life goal that would gradually move up their 'to do' list as the years passed.

To her huge credit Lorraine can prove that ideas put in her mental pending tray don't tend to be forgotten. However happy-go-lucky and relaxed she appears to be on screen, her track record shows that she ultimately achieves all her goals. On the career front she doesn't tread on people or behave badly in order to get ahead – as proven by the near total absence of fellow professionals who will criticise her even when they are promised anonymity. What gets Lorraine ahead is a combination of hard work and persistence. When she sets her mind to something she follows through. If she needs new skills she will learn them and if she needs to practise she will do so. But in the end she tends to prevail.

So while it might sound crazy, few people who know her are betting against her achieving her next, extraordinary goal. Running marathons and doing midnight walks were old hat. Now, closer to fifty than to forty, Lorraine started to make plans to drag a sledge a hundred miles across the Antarctic to the South Pole.

20

NEW CHALLENGE

*'I think that a lot of us get bogged down and
somewhere along the line lose the will to dream and
to be happy about wee daft things.'*

'Is it because I was brought up in East Kilbride? I don't
know. But for some reason I've always been drawn to
frozen parts and cold places,' Lorraine says when asked about
her new dream. 'Going to Alaska a few years ago and seeing
bears and whales, and going dog sledging on a glacier was one
of the best holidays I have ever had. I have a fascination with
everything related to Antarctica. If I hadn't been a journalist,
or my second most likely job of a teacher, then I would have
loved to have been an explorer or a traveller. I've been into
explorers ever since I was a little girl.'

The girl who dreamed of becoming a fighter pilot also
defied sexual stereotyping by being obsessively into maps. She
stuck a huge map of Antarctica on the wall of her home office
in Berkshire and ensured it made it up to Scotland when they
moved. Gazing at it when she was stuck for words on her
newspaper column, or needed a break from the research for a
new television show always left her feeling inspired. She says

she sat glued to the television when the award-winning Channel 4 drama *Shackleton* was broadcast, with Kenneth Branagh playing the lead role and acting out the adventure she had been reading and dreaming about for years.

In 1907, long before Captain Scott completed the journey, Ernest Shackleton and a team of two dozen crew members embarked on an expedition to Antarctica and made it to within one hundred miles of the South Pole, nearly dying in the process. They had got closer than anyone else, but were beaten back when they ran out of food and realised they would have to return to base or die on the ice. 'I thought you would prefer a live donkey than a dead lion,' Shackleton reportedly told his wife on his return.

This was just one of the many famous phrases associated with the man. The simplest, 'Difficulties are just things to be overcome', was the one that helped make him a lifelong hero to Lorraine. So, nearly a century after his voyage, she decided she would try to finish the job for him. She wanted to walk those final hundred miles. Those closest to her accepted the news in silence. 'Steve and Rosie think I am mad anyway so it didn't surprise them when I told them what I was hoping to do,' Lorraine says. And the more she thought about it, the keener she became. She knew she would have to follow the advice which had served her well all her life, the philosophy which had so inspired her grandmother: stop dreaming and start doing.

So Lorraine got on the phone. She tracked down a succession of experts to find out whether it would indeed be practical or even possible for her to trek across those hundred miles. The answers were always the same: yes, you can, but you will be suffering every step of the way. As part of her private research she met up with Michael McGrath, a man with muscular dystrophy, who shared her fascination with the polar explorers and had just finished two incredible journeys to the North and South Poles. He could hardly have inspired her more, but could Lorraine really follow his example?

The experts said the safest time is in our winter, the Antarctic summer when temperatures can be as 'warm' as minus 20 [degrees symbol closed up] C. Lorraine knew she would have to be fitter than ever if she were to survive it. She was told she needed to get used to attaching a tractor tyre to her body and dragging it along the ground for two miles at a time because on the trek to the Pole she would be dragging everything she needed for the journey on a sledge. At first, she planned to start training with a smile – she worked out she could pull Rosie along on the back of a wheeled sledge as practice. But she knew that if she was ever to do the journey for real she would need to get serious. 'If I do it then it will be the most ambitious thing I have ever done and the training will be serious. Just like my marathons, I won't be out to break any records. I know this is dangerous for me and for the team so I will be very, very sensible. I just want to complete the journey. I think that it's the idea of pitting yourself against yourself that appeals. You're only against you.'

As the plans became more serious, Lorraine joined forces with an eight-person team headed by polar explorer Fiona Thornewill. There were hopes that Christmas 2006 could be a possible date for the trip, though in the event the trek, which aimed to raise huge amounts of money for the National Osteoporosis Society and the MS Charitable Trust, was put back a year for logistical reasons. If they didn't go in 2007, then Lorraine vowed she would make the trek in 2009, to coincide with her fiftieth birthday.

In the meantime she had got used to hearing people mock her plans. Cynics who knew nothing about her seemed to feel it was ridiculous to think a breakfast television presenter could rough it and survive such a journey. But they didn't realise just how often Lorraine had defied the odds before. When they told her she could never work on television with her Scottish accent, she proved them wrong. When they said she couldn't present a show while heavily pregnant, she proved them wrong. When they said she didn't have the mental or physical strength to run marathons, she proved them wrong. She swore she would do the same with Antarctica.

And even if logistical problems meant the trip was postponed again, what was so wrong with having an extraordinary goal? Making plans made life better, she argued. They could make life worthwhile. 'I think that a lot of us get bogged down and somewhere along the line lose the will to dream and to be happy about wee daft things,' she said, when she was asked why she was so determined to follow in Shackleton's footsteps. 'I know a lot of people live really shitty lives – I interview them all the time. But I think we have just got to keep moving on and to take the joy out of what we can because you never know what's around the corner.'

Lorraine Kelly swore she would never stop dreaming, never stop achieving.

* * * * *

'Hi, my name's Lorraine. What's yours?'

It was just before 1pm one Friday lunchtime in late 2006 and Lorraine had walked into a restaurant in Dundee and approached a lone man sitting with a drink at the bar. Glancing at herself very quickly in one of the restaurant's mirrors, she allowed herself a smile. She had spent some time getting ready for this secret assignation – and she thought she looked pretty good. The man at the bar certainly seemed to approve. He smiled, introduced himself, shook her hand and gestured that she should join him. After chatting for a while and ordering herself a drink Lorraine then followed him to a discrete table for two in the far corner of the room.

With her television work done for the week she was able to relax as her companion looked at the wine list. She was on a date – and the man sitting opposite her was her husband Steve.

'We try and do this every few weeks, setting aside a Friday lunchtime when we will meet as if it is for the first time,' she says, thrilled that after twenty-one years together they are still as happy as ever. The good news extends from hotel restaurants right into the bedroom, she was happy to tell *Heat* magazine when she gave one of her latest, no-holds-barred interviews. 'Sex? It actually gets better. It's all about the boobies with Steve. Lots of boobie-feeling goes on. He still fancies me.' Too much information, you might have thought, but Lorraine wasn't finished. 'What a winkie! I'm very happy in that department, thank you,' she said, as she laughed like a drain with her interviewer and made a fair few people blush back in Dundee.

Lorraine was hugely proud that her marriage was still so strong. They had beaten the curse of the cameraman – the unwritten rule that relationships between presenters and crew are doomed to failure. But both Lorraine and Steve work hard to stay happy. 'Often with marriages you take each other for granted, especially if you've got kids. You have to make time just for each other. And fortunately Steve still makes me laugh. We have fun together.' As well as their Friday night dates the pair also try to head off for long weekends in Scotland, Europe or further afield a few times a year. 'We have just got back from Grenada in the Caribbean – but we did spend most of the time talking about Rosie,' she says of their most recent adult-only mini-break. She also jokes about the number of times hotel receptionists recognise her and look aghast, thinking she is having an affair, because she and Steve always book in under their married name, the deeply suspicious-sounding Mr and Mrs Smith.

At home Lorraine has had plenty of practice at being a super-mum. Rosie now has dozens of close friends in Dundee and few weekends go by without two or three of them coming round for all-day parties and sleepovers. In the week Lorraine is also a vital part of the local mums' mafia, pitching in and picking up their kids from school, and looking after them whenever required. It was a workload that *Sunday Times* reporter Anna Burnside says was too exhausting to contemplate.

'You clearly think I am mad,' Lorraine remarked to Anna after explaining her daily routines. But it wasn't really Lorraine that Anna was thinking of.

'I didn't have the heart to tell her that I was simply intrigued by the other mothers, who are so busy they have to ask a marathon-running, show-prerecording, Dundee to London commuting, Royal Television Society Presenter Of The Year to pick up their kids,' she said afterwards.

For Lorraine, family life and friends were so important that any extra effort was worth making. Her mum, though biased, says she is hugely proud of her daughter's kindness. Lorraine might be paid to talk, but Anne says that in private she is a wonderful listener. Over the years she says she has lost count of the ways Lorraine tries to put others at their ease. 'If we are out and if there is ever anyone in a room who looks lonely she will go over and speak to them. She is a very loyal friend as well,' Anne said with pride.

Joyce, Lorraine's oldest friend, is equally proud to know her. 'I know we will always be friends, whatever happens in life. I like to think of us in our dotage, sitting on a beach in Majorca having a good natter. What's more, I think we will!'

For her part, Lorraine says she hopes that the happy old woman on the Majorcan beach will have aged in as dignified a manner as possible. Now closer to 50 than 40, she is increasingly comfortable with the way she looks. She is even happy having her photo taken. 'I don't mind having wrinkles and sags because it gives me character – I certainly don't think I would go under the knife for anything that wasn't life-threatening,' she said, after several of her contemporaries had 'work' carried out on their faces to try and push back time. 'Some women who have had facelifts look like they've been in a wind tunnel, and in America you see all those breasts looking like Exocet missiles on the beach. I just don't see how people can think that looks attractive. I don't think I could actually go through with an operation. I don't do pain and I'd just be too scared of ending up looking like a Klingon.' In truth, she has more reasons than most to fear plastic surgery gone wrong. Steve recently worked on a show about cosmetic procedures and he and Lorraine saw plenty of impossible-to-broadcast footage that put them both off surgery for life.

'A good bra and moisturiser is far cheaper anyway,' she

concludes with a smile. More importantly, she reckons the key is to feel happy in your own skin – whatever it looks like. 'Women say things like: When I lose a stone, everything will be fabulous. Or everything will be fine if I have a boob job. But the fact is that everything will be the same – you will just be a wee bit thinner or have perter boobies. If you think you will have a face lift and come out looking like Michelle Pfeiffer, you won't. You need to focus on what you feel like in yourself.'

For Lorraine, this means knowing exactly who you are and trying to live your life by the best rules. 'I'm a great believer in what goes around comes around. If you are nasty and bitchy it will show in your face and your personality, and it will come back and bite your bum. I'm not saying I'm Pollyanna – I can swear, lose my temper and be tetchy – but, essentially, I try to live my life in a decent way,' she says.

That's exactly why she was able to shake off two potential career crises towards the end of 2006. The first came when the *LK Today* team were out on a gruelling shoot in Namibia and producer Benedetta Pinelli wrote a text message to her husband – and mistakenly sent it to Lorraine herself. The words were damning. 'I have had a massive bust-up with LK. She is a nightmare to work with. I hate her,' Bernedetta typed. As it turned out, the reasons for Benedetta's anger was professional, not personal – there had been a disagreement over how an item was to be filmed, with Lorraine convinced she knew best what GMTV viewers would want to watch. GMTV appeared to agree. Benedetta resigned from her job within days, and with GMTV's full backing the Namibia shows were aired exactly as Lorraine had imagined them.

The next minor problem came when Lorraine gave a speech

to seven-hundred new students at Dundee University. 'Just have a fantastic time. I know you are here to work hard, but play hard as well. Study hard, play hard, drink lots and have safe sex,' she said. In truth it was both a realistic and responsible comment, but plenty of people lined up to say it sent out all the wrong messages. Lorraine was forced on the defensive and said that she apologised to anyone she had inadvertently offended.

Fortunately, for all the ups and downs, she ended 2006 smiling. Lorraine was put in third place behind Charlotte Church and Kelly Brook in a 'best real boobs in showbiz' poll. 'This is especially gratifying as it turns out that mine are actually older than both of their perky pairs combined,' Lorraine wrote in her *Sun* column, almost laughing out loud as she typed. Three weeks later she was laughing again, when her specially decorated bra sold for £1,100 more than Jordan's at an auction raising funds for breast cancer. At forty six she could still give sex symbols half her age a serious run for their money – and it felt fantastic.

This year, as she looks forward to her forty-eighth birthday, her fifteenth wedding anniversary and the start of her twenty-fifth year on television Lorraine Kelly is still ready to take on whatever new challenges come her way. If she succeeds, she will be thrilled. And if she fails, she will laugh, put it down to experience and move on to something else. What she won't do is stagnate, feel sorry for herself or forget how lucky she is.

'Don't save for best. Today is best.'

That's what Lorraine always remembers her grandmother saying – Granny Mac, who wore bright red lipstick and free-flowing clothes on even the darkest of days. If someone gave her lovely perfume she would spray herself all over even if she was only going to take the rubbish out. 'I've always liked that philosophy. Squeeze every last drop out of every day and make every moment as special as you can.' Of all the advice she has ever been given, Lorraine says these words still mean the most. She has always tried to make every moment special – and she won't stop now.